NIGERIA
GIANT OF AFRICA

NIGERIA
GIANT OF AFRICA

PETER HOLMES

ACKNOWLEDGEMENTS

I would like to thank the Federal Department of Antiquities for permission to republish the photographs on pages 75, 83, 87, 132 and 159. These all appeared in the excellent book *Two Thousand Year Nigerian Art* (Lagos 1977), by Dr Ekpo Eyo, the Director-General of the Federal Department.

I also express thanks to the Gulf Oil Company for permission to publish the two photographs on page 86; to Chris Christodolo for permission to publish the photograph on page 185; and to Rod Rea for permission to publish the photograph on page 69.

The remaining photographs in this book are among the many thousands I took while in Nigeria. These are held by the J. Allan Cash Photolibrary in London.

In my travels around Nigeria and in my research for this book I was helped by many people, too numerous to mention. But I would especially like to thank Dr Arinze of the Federal Department of Antiquities; Alhaji Mohammad Kyari, a Director of the Nigerian Tobacco Company; and Dr Alastair Lamb of Roxford, England.

The design of this book owes much to Laurence Bradbury. Barbara Baylis and Martha Holmes assisted with the book's preparation; Freddie Mansfield with photographic organization; my wife Judy Holmes with research, the large red pencil and all-round support. Michael Rainbird and Mary Anne Sanders of The Oregon Press provided both expertise and patience.

Finally, I would like to thank the National Oil and Chemical Marketing Company of Nigeria, without whose sponsorship this book would not have been possible.

First published in Great Britain in 1985 by
The Oregon Press Limited, Faraday House,
8–10 Charing Cross Road, London WC2H OHG

Design: Laurence Bradbury

Phototypeset by Falcon Graphic Art Limited, Wallington, Surrey
Printed and bound by Springbourne Press Limited,
Basildon, Essex, England

ISBN 0 9508498 1 2

Half title: Marriage pot from Bida,
Niger State

Frontispiece: Fisherman on
Sokoto River

Opposite: Village in fertile
countryside, just north of the
Niger River, near Bida, Niger
State

CONTENTS

PREFACE

On 1 October 1985, Nigeria will celebrate the twenty-fifth year of its Independence. The Silver Jubilee, marking as it does the passing of a generation, cannot but give pause for reflection on the changes and progress that time has wrought. From the balanced society and civilizations of the past, our country is growing to modern nationhood, full of hope but with tensions and the severe competitive stresses of industrialization.

Ours is a busy world in which local events are often no longer understood either by Nigerians or by visitors. This is because we are not completely attuned to our changing society; nor are we sufficiently aware of its history and the economic, social, political and spiritual factors that help form it.

This book sets out to portray Nigeria as it really is: a country blessed with enormous natural resources, a great variety of cultures and beauty of which Nigerians can be proud. It also reminds us vividly that we have much to preserve from our past and much to protect in the way of natural beauty. This should be our increasing concern in years to come.

The petroleum industry has been in the forefront of industrialization, and by the nature of its operations it has a special responsibility in these directions. It is therefore with very special appreciation that I welcome this book in the name of the National Oil & Chemical Marketing Company, since the author, Peter Holmes, is already well known in Nigeria as a former Chief Executive of Shell Petroleum Development Company; he continues to demonstrate a keen interest in our arts and cultural heritage.

Readers will quickly become aware that a wide range of interests, an historian's bent, and an eager camera's eye, qualify him well to present us to ourselves in 1985. It will be a dull mind that is not stimulated and a cold heart that does not find fresh understanding from these pages.

I am delighted and proud to introduce this book to a wide public and to promote knowledge and awareness of Nigeria among our many friends.

M.O. AKANBI
General Manager and Chief Executive
National Oil and Chemical Marketing Company

Opposite: Lagos harbour at sunset

Overleaf: Niger Valley near
Koton-Karifi, Kwara State

FOREWORD

Nigeria, Giant of Africa is a Silver Jubilee tribute with a difference. Its author and photographer Peter Holmes read History at Cambridge, learned Arabic and worked in various capacitites for Shell in the Arab world before coming to Nigeria. He is thus undoubtedly equipped to view the country not from the standpoint of oil alone. To an acute perception and an unusual historical insight he has added skill in photography; the result is that he has given us a truly remarkable book, a befitting commemoration of twenty-five years of Nigeria's independence.

He has captured for us in striking pictures the ingredients of Nigeria's potential greatness as an African country: the diversity of its people and the many facets of their life; the richness of its environment in flora and fauna; its efforts at development and glimpses of the complexities of oil exploration. The book sheds unmistakable light on Nigeria, portraying its beauties by taking the reader on a grand tour of this lively country.

It is, however, in the historical introduction which illuminates this pictorial book that Peter Holmes has truly distinguished himself. He has shown such a remarkable grasp of the problems of unfolding the history of Africa that he must be placed in the vanguard of the 'new historians' who believe that the Africans had a history before the coming of the Europeans. It is refreshing to see him demolishing the notion that Nigeria, christened by Flora Shaw (later Lady Lugard), was a mere geographical expression, the result of the European imperial rivalries that delineated its boundaries at the Berlin Conference of 1884. Using Arab written sources, the accounts of explorers and traders (and, one may add, missionaries), and admitting the validity of oral traditions as well as the value of archaeological materials, the author is able to relate the ancient Kanem-Bornu Kingdom, the Sokoto (Fulani) Caliphate, the Oyo and Benin Empires as well as the smaller societies in the Igbo areas (and one might also add the trading houses of the Niger Delta) and show that they represented indigenous political organisations whose importance to the development of Nigeria cannot be ignored. Culturally, through the Nok figurines of the Benue region, the Igbo-Ukwu art objects, to the Ife terracottas and Benin bronzes, and onwards to the Owo masterpieces, there runs a certain artistic continuum in the Nigerian cultural heritage of at least 2000 years.

The upshot of all this is that the diverse people of Nigeria inhabited lively polities before the Europeans came; they traded among themselves and beyond their borders before the advent of the slave trade and, where they were not literate in Arabic, they enshrined their history in oral forms. Beneath their diversity there lay a certain element of unity and with the evolution of the colonial period there emerged a Federation which a Civil War has further consolidated, for no unit can now secede.

The task before Nigeria is one of development; to eliminate ignorance, poverty and disease. Undoubtedly, Nigeria is a giant awakening (and this book has demonstrated that unmistakably). That is the essence of this tribute on the occasion of Nigeria's Jubilee of Independence. The response from Nigerians, however, must be to build upon their inherent unity of culture and purpose; to save our country by our determined exertions and to save Africa, our Continent, by our progressive example.

DR SABURI BIOBAKU C.M.G

Opposite: Sunset over Tangale Hill, Bauchi State

ESSAY

When I was a student at Cambridge we took a course called 'The Expansion of Europe' in which we learned, among other things, that Africa in the latter part of the 19th century and the first years of the present century was divided up among the various colonial powers, Britain, France, Germany, Portugal and Italy. This process, the course implied, took place without the consent of the indigenous African peoples; and it produced divisions within the continent that were based not on the facts of history but on the convenience of the colonial powers, a convenience often derived from considerations of non-African origin. One such state, we were told, was Nigeria, the very name of which was thought up by the wife-to-be of Lord Lugard, that very epitome of proconsul of Empire. The boundaries of Nigeria were determined by negotiations between the French, the British and the Germans, and, so the argument runs, the Nigeria that became independent in 1960 was in a very significant way a creation of the rivalries and the relationships of those three European powers.

When I finally came to live and work in Nigeria I soon realized that this view, while it contained one or two germs of truth, was in fact so superficial as to be virtually insignificant. It is true that the physical boundaries of Nigeria to the west, to the north and to the east (with one exception) were defined in the colonial period by the colonial powers concerned. These boundaries, however, served to confine, as it were, an already existing history that extended back long long before the coming of the Europeans; and in a surprising way the establishment of the boundaries of Nigeria does really reflect the historical background of pre-Nigerian civilizations, states and cultures. The point, in fact, is well represented by that exception already mentioned on the eastern boundary of Nigeria where the present limits do not coincide precisely with those established by the pre-independence colonial regimes. What happened here was that a very artificial border, drawn in the late 19th century between Germany and Britain defining certain spheres of influence in the hinterland, proved at the time of independence to be quite untenable. The people of a portion of British Cameroun, which in itself was a partition of the former German colony of Kamerun, voted by plebiscite shortly after Nigerian independence to join Nigeria rather than the newly emerging Republic of Cameroun. This was because their traditional links, both cultural and ethnic, lay so much more with Nigeria than they did with the new state to which it was proposed they should now attach themselves. These links were the consequence of the fact that the northern part of Cameroun was involved in a historical process with what was to become the northern part of Nigeria, a historical process that dated back at

Opposite above: Kano, drawn by Heinrich Barth in 1850

Opposite below: Muglebu, just south of Mubi, Gongola State, in 1851

least to the opening years of the 19th century and long before any British colonial administration appeared on the scene.

The example of the 1961 plebiscite relating to the northern part of what was once British Cameroun is but one rather dramatic example of a phenomenon that permeates the whole of Nigeria. Despite the multitudes of languages, the apparent complications of ethnic groups, the divisions of religion, there exist, and have existed for a very long time, common threads connecting the various parts that make up the modern state of Nigeria today in such a way that it is not easy to imagine them existing in another combination. My purpose in these introductory remarks is to point out and comment briefly on some of the main themes that I felt, during my years in Nigeria, were dominating influences in giving to the modern state of Nigeria this characteristic which can only be described as Nigerian.

There are many problems in the study of the history of the territory that makes up Nigeria which are not to be found in the usual European western state, and are only now beginning to be solved by a new generation of scholars who have grown up in an independent Nigeria and in the benevolent atmosphere of the large number of universities and other academic institutions that have arisen since 1960.

One of the major problems confronting anyone wishing to know more about the history of Nigeria, particularly of Nigeria before the arrival of the Euopeans, is the nature of the source material available. As I understand it, there are four fairly well recognized sources for the study of Nigeria and West African history in general. Many of these present problems to the student that are of quite a different kind to those presented, say, to the English student of the history of England. The first source category is that of works written in Arabic, or in non-Arabic languages but using the Arabic script (more often the former than the latter). From the years that the Islamic Arab Empire spread onto the north shore of Africa in the middle of the 7th century AD Arab scholars, geographers, historians and ethnographers began to show great interest in the lands to the south, particularly the lands that lay across the great Sahara desert. As trans-Saharan trade grew in volume throughout the last centuries of the Middle Ages so did the volume of information reaching Arab scholars increase, and the later Arab sources are extremely detailed in many aspects of sub-Saharan history. It is from them that we know the stories of the great West African empires of Ghana and Mali, Songhai and the like. The sources in this category throw a great deal of light upon the early history of northern Nigeria, both on the early history of Hausa states such as Katsina, Kano and Zazzau (Zaria), and also on one of the great early sub-Saharan empires of West Africa, Kanem-Borno.

The Kanem-Borno Empire has its roots in the century or so immediately following the Arab conquest and is therefore one of the world's oldest states. At one time it extended from the shores of Lake Chad almost across the Sahara to the Murzuk oasis in what is today southern Libya. By the end of the 15th century, however, the main centre of gravity of Kanem-Borno had shifted to that region not far removed from the modern town of Maiduguri. A surprising amount is known historically about Kanem-Borno because of the existence of Arabic language or Arabic script records. The translations of documents published by H. R. Palmer in his *Sudanese Memoirs* are a sample of the wealth of material relating to Kanem-Borno that exists in this particular medium. Having studied Arabic myself and spent a great deal of my career before coming to Nigeria in Arabic-speaking countries, I must confess that I was particularly fascinated by this kind of source material.

The existence of this Arabic source material, which is increasingly being studied by scholars in Nigeria and elsewhere, arises in the main from two factors. First, Islam, which reached the shores of North Africa in the latter part of the 7th century AD, began very soon afterwards to spread across the Sahara to the states that lay to the south; and inevitably, with the spread of Islam and its emphasis upon the Koran, came the spread of Arabic language and Arabic scholarship. This was a two-way process. Islam and Arabic ideas penetrated into the African continent. Information about Africa spread northwards across the Sahara into those regions where it could be recorded by Arabs or Arabic-speaking scholars. Second, the mechanism that brought these influences to and fro across the Sahara lay in an ever-increasing connection between the Black African states of the southern Sudan and the Islamic southern shores of the Mediterranean, based on the trans-Saharan caravan trade. This trade was extremely complicated in that it concerned not only the states on either side of the Sahara, but also the nomadic populations within the Sahara itself; and it often involved the transport of goods and people over what must be acknowledged as very long distances by the laborious traditional methods of the camel caravan. Although much of this trade has today disappeared, nevertheless the diligent observer of northern Nigeria can still find evidence that aspects of it have survived, and on a quite large scale. One fascinating example is the trade in Turkudi veils, which are woven in very narrow strips, then sewn together and dyed a deep indigo blue, which is subsequently beaten again and again to produce a profound sheen. All these processes are carried out in a number of villages in and around Kano. The complete veils and other cotton garments similarly dyed and beaten are exported all over the Sahara. One important outlet for the Kano Turkudi veils is the central Saharan town of Agadez, several hundred miles to the north; but Turkudi veils originating from the Kano area can be found in nomad markets all over the Sahara as far west as the Atlantic coast. This trade in the manufacture and distribution of these garments, for which the desert nomads will pay very high prices indeed, has its roots in a period a thousand years old and it has gone on in almost exactly the same way until the present. Here is but one living example of the ancient trans-Saharan caravan trade about which the Arab geographers of the Middle Ages have told us so much.

Far more accessible to the person educated in European languages are documents originating from western contacts with West Africa, which began in the latter years of the 15th century. At first these were predominantly Portuguese, but subsequently we have added to them sources in English, Dutch, French, Spanish and even German and Danish. Initially the records of trade and traders were restricted to activities along the coast. By the beginning of the 19th century sources of this kind began to give us information of what was going on further and further into the hinterland. By the middle of the 19th century – which saw, for example, the great journeys of the German, Heinrich Barth – knowledge provided by exploring missions had covered much of the country from the coast of Nigeria through into the Sahara beyond what are today the northern boundaries of the country. Many of these travel accounts are beautifully produced and admirably written by travellers who were extremely observant and who did their best to illustrate what they saw not only in words but also in pictures. There is, however, one obvious defect in this body of literature: it is written by Europeans and it is dominated by a European point of view. Acute observation is no substitute for a deep knowledge of a traditional way of life. These early travel accounts of the 19th century tell us a great deal, but equally there are many things on which they are silent and about which we would dearly love to know a great deal more. Moreover, there were many parts of what is today Nigeria that were visited by no 19th-century traveller, and many parts that were visited by travellers who left no written record.

To the travel accounts, in many cases attractive and readable, must be added a multitude of more mundane sources. Notable among these are the records of the colonial administration that began to proliferate in the latter part of the 19th century, and in the present century developed into a mass of valuable data. These records have survived to a very great extent and have provided a mine of information for scholars to work away at for many years to come.

In pre-colonial Nigeria there were many states of a political sophistication and degree of organization which were at the same time either non-literate, that is to say of a culture not in the habit of expressing itself in the form of writing, or with access only to the literate abilities of other civilizations, whether Arab or European. Since many of these states are extremely important to the understanding of Nigeria today, historians have naturally tried to find other means than those of the written word to work out the nature of their histories. One technique of great importance has been developed that depends on what is generally known as the oral tradition: that is to say, the understanding of how the people themselves, either at the level of the ruler and his court or in the form of folklore, legend and myth, see their own past. Oral tradition is a fascinating field of study because it contains a component that is absent from the normal archival records so common in the states of Europe and America. It is possible – and there are many examples, not only in Nigeria but in other parts of Africa – to have an official history recorded purely by an oral tradition method. You can have an official 'rememberer' of the past who records in some form of verse or song, perhaps accompanied by drums or other musical instruments, the official records of the history of the people.

As we might expect, this sort of record usually preserves what recorders wish to preserve; it has the delightful property that, should a king be singularly unsuccessful or an event be especially disastrous, it is possible simply to decide to forget it. A forgotten event in an oral tradition-style history is one that never took place at all and just disappears from the records for ever. When working out chronological lists of kings, for example, from oral tradition sources, this kind of point must always be borne in mind. There may well be kings so disastrous that it has been decided unanimously to drop them from the 'memory' and they have not survived even in name. It also happens quite often that the king lists of minor states tend to copy those of the dominant state of the region, perhaps out of politeness, perhaps out of the simple convenience of using somebody else's list as a basic framework for chronology.

Problems of this kind make an oral tradition-based history look rather different from one that depends on written documents. Nevertheless, the history so produced is real history and it contains a wealth of information about the past of a people. It would be foolish indeed to dismiss it as the mere collecting of folklore. Much of our knowledge about the various Yoruba states, of enormous importance from the late Middle Ages onwards, and whose role in Nigerian history can hardly be overestimated, is derived from sources of this kind. If we want to work out the historical background of those regions that were not visited either by Arab speakers or Europeans in the 19th century and therefore left no record in the first two source types that we have discussed, then some form of oral tradition approach is the only way we are going to find out anything at all. A particular problem in dealing with source material of the oral tradition type is that it may well show a lack of internal consistency. In other words, you may find several versions that in fact conflict with each other. There are, for example, at least two quite distinct legends as to the origin of the Yoruba people: in one they originate from a single point in what is today Nigeria, namely Ile Ife; in the other the ancestors of the Yoruba migrate from somewhere else, perhaps quite a long way away, pushed on by defeat in war or some other such pressure and arriving at Ile Ife from whence the whole structure of Yoruba state evolution begins. This duality of origin is not uncommon in other parts of West Africa and it may well in itself represent an important historical truth, namely that the people concerned had both a long prehistory of migration and unsettled life, and later a profound association with a particular place or region which became to them the centre of their religious and temporal existences. These two elements do not in fact conflict with each other.

In recent years a further source of knowledge concerning the Nigerian past has been exploited on an ever-increasing scale. This is the use of archaeological methods of investigation. Scientific archaeology is a fairly recent development in any part of the world, and in Nigeria it has only been exploited on a significant scale over the last few decades, and particularly in the years following Independence in 1960. However, evidence of an archaeological or semi-archaeological nature has been known since at least the latter part of the 19th century. This indicated the early civilization in Nigeria was of a far higher level of attainment than might have generally been assumed. The revelations of the artistic treasures of Benin, particularly in bronzes produced by the *cire perdu* (lost wax) process, which were made at the end of the 19th century, were amplified shortly afterwards by the discovery of even more sophisticated objects of art in the shape of bronzes and other sculptures from Ife. Rightly they are regarded as among the greatest of the nation's treasures. To these have been added in recent years a large number of other artistic complexes of which perhaps the most interesting is the so-called Nok culture which came to light soon after the end of World War II. Bernard Fagg, one of the pioneers in the study of Nok, is of the view that a better term for this would be the Benue civilization, because these extraordinary terracotta heads and other objects – again, as in the case of Ife, of extraordinary beauty – are distributed along a large part of the Benue Valley from the confluence towards the present border with Cameroun.

In recent years archaeology has been exploited more systematically. There have been excavations in Benin, in Ife, and in a number of sites of which the most dramatic, perhaps, were those known collectively as Igbo-Ukwu. The Igbo-Ukwu excavations have brought to light a mass of material, including yet another collection of bronze sculptures produced by the lost wax process; these are stylistically different from Ife, yet of both great antiquity and extraordinary sophistication. (These Igbo-Ukwu discoveries have also shown that state formation on a scale comparable to that of, for example, the Yoruba states in the 17th and 18th centuries, was a process that extended far more to the east than has hitherto been generally supposed.)

To these four sources of information about Nigerian history we might perhaps add a fifth. There is nowhere in Nigeria where the intelligent observer cannot see evidence of that process of change which is history; the evolution from past to present, from traditional and ancient to modern and technological. One can see ceremonies and traditions that have their roots in a distant past; towns that have moved from one site to another as a result of past conflicts; court ceremonial and systems of administration that antedate by centuries the coming of the British and the other colonial powers; architectural traditions that precede by many centuries the civilization of post-Renaissance Europe.

However, in order to understand contemporary Nigeria, it is necessary to have some feeling for the evolution of events which produced the country that achieved independence in 1960. In order to do this we must touch upon at least some of the main trends of events, and categories of event, which make up the raw material of Nigerian history.

Nigeria divides itself conveniently from a geographical point of view into three sections, defined by the Y-shaped formation of the River Niger and its tributary the Benue. To the north of the Niger–Benue confluence lies the savannah country leading towards the Sahara; and it is here that over the centuries the Islamic states of the Hausa and Kanem-Borno Empire evolved and existed. It is also here, of course, that one of the most dramatic events of recent Nigerian history, the rise of the Fulani Empire in the early 19th century, also had its origin.

On the south-western side of this 'Y', south and west of the Niger below the Niger–Benue confluence, there lies an area in which at least from the 14th century, and probably earlier, there existed a number of clearly defined states with centralized policies controlled by chiefs or other forms of hereditary kingship assisted by a well-established and elaborate system of bureaucratic administration, with an extension of that administration into the regions to form some kind of imperial relationship between one state and another. When the Europeans first came to West Africa in the late 15th century there were a number of states of this kind in the process of expansion in the region that stretches along the forest tracks of the West African coast between the Atlantic to the south and the savannah states to the north. The arrival of the Europeans, which opened up a fresh commercial outlet in the shape of trade to the south to add to the more traditional commercial connections of trade to the north, greatly accelerated the development of these states, so that by the 17th century they were very rapidly turning into extremely powerful entities which were greatly respected and frequently feared and watched with great anxiety by the European traders in their forts and settlements along the coast.

By 1700 there were the Yoruba states centred around Oyo, with to the east the kingdom of Benin, which was similar in structure and organization to these states. To the west there was the state of Dahomey, again structurally analogous to Yoruba states such as Oyo. To the north of these lay yet further states but very little understood, because of their remoteness from the European observers on the coast who are an important source for this period. Examples of such states are Nupe, whose last capital, Bida, is still a fascinating reminder of the magnitude of Nigerian history; and Borgu. To the north of these in turn lay the Islamicized Hausa states to which reference has already been made, and which gave access to the caravan routes of the Sahara; and to their east lay Borno, likewise engaged intimately in the trans-Saharan trade.

On the eastern half of this Y-shaped river formation, which includes the Niger delta and the Benue from the point of its confluence with the Niger eastwards, there exists a situation in terms of history which is far more complex and little understood. In much of this area there were populations who belonged to the category sometimes referred to as 'non-centralized societies'. What is meant here is the system of social organization based on lineage, the village and other small localities rather than the elaborate and formalized structures of kingship and bureaucratic administration that we have seen developing among, for example, the Yoruba in Oyo. Many of these non-centralized states or societies were very small both in area and in population. Others, probably, were rather larger than has hitherto been supposed, and may indeed have enjoyed structures of administration not too far removed from the centralized Yoruba and Benin model. Certainly, the discoveries at Igbo-Ukwu suggest a royal form of administration in a region which had hitherto been regarded as being very much the preserve of societies that did not as a rule have single supreme chiefs with authority over all their subjects. Moreover, some of the peoples in this region, for example the Jukun, show political structures that could very easily have evolved into something analogous to the centralized states to the west. A similar phenomenon, although perhaps at a much earlier stage of evolution, probably existed eastwards into the mountainous territory that was to become part of German, and then British, Cameroun, where again a highly structured scheme of chiefly rule existed not on an imperial scale but as a multitude of small chieftains. Small, however, did not mean lack of political sophistication or structure. Whatever may have been the political patterns extant over the past centuries in this south-eastern corner of Nigeria, in terms of their impact on the broad scale of Nigerian history, however, and in particular on the pattern of British penetration, they are relatively less important.

The dramatic advance of British colonial rule into Nigeria and the events that were to lead in 1914 to the formation of a Nigerian Federation, from which Nigeria in 1960 emerged as an independent sovereign state, were dominated by two main factors. First, there was the process of disturbance and conflict leading to the collapse of the states to the west of the lower Niger, those of the Yoruba and then of Benin. Second, there was the extraordinarily rapid expansion of a new power in the north of what today is Nigeria, but in the early 19th century was a region with a multitude of small Hausa states. This was the rise of the Fulani Empire by the process of the *jihad* of Uthman dan Fodio.

When at the end of the 15th century the Portuguese reached the coast of the state of Benin, already in the hinterland there was emerging the nucleus of a Yoruba imperial structure. Based on Oyo, this power was not to approach maturity until the 17th century when, at last free from attacks from the north from Nupe, Oyo was able to begin a process of what was to amount, in the 18th century, to imperial expansion on a most impressive scale. It has been argued that it was the rise of the slave trade upon the Atlantic coast that provided the economic infrastructure for the Yoruba Empire of Oyo in the 18th century. This is certainly a serious oversimplification. Although the arrival of European trade along the coast from the end of the 15th century greatly stimulated economic activity in the hinterland, there can be no doubt that there were many other factors at work, not least the expansion of trade with the savannah states and into and across the Sahara to North Africa. It is often forgotten that the 16th century not only saw a great increase of commercial activity stimulated by the expansion of Europe along the coast of West Africa but also, in the Mediterranean, an equally significant rise in the tempo of economic activity stimulated by a multitude of factors such as the Renaissance in southern Europe and the rise of the Ottoman empire in Turkey and its expansion along the shores of North Africa. By the latter part of the 18th century the rulers of Oyo, known as the Alafin, had extended their influence to the coast to include what is now the metropolis of Lagos and also the kingdom of Dahomey (which today is the nucleus of the People's Republic of Benin). At this point Oyo was probably the largest of all the kingdoms along the West African coast, and perhaps the most powerful, even greater than the contemporary empire of Ashanti. There appear, however, to have been weaknesses at the centre of Oyo administration. By the end of the 18th century the Empire was in decline and early in the 19th century it rapidly began to disintegrate. Oyo tributaries including Dahomey broke away in the south. Some notionally remained part of the Empire, but to all intents and purposes ignored its rule. Others like Dahomey ceased to acknowledge any part of it at all. At the same time within Oyo itself rebellion broke out and there were in the first decades of the 19th century a series of civil wars which culminated in about 1836 in the abandonment of the town of Oyo itself.

The centre of Yoruba power moved to Ibadan and a host of new towns like Abeokuta and Ogbomosho were founded either by warring factions or by settlement of Yoruba refugees fleeing the chaos of civil war. Several of these new towns, originally temporary strongholds or places of refuge, have evolved into some of the largest cities in Nigeria. Ibadan, which was a product of this period, is now one of the biggest cities in the whole continent of Africa. The old Yoruba towns often occupied very large areas of country and were less towns than widely scattered expanses of settlement surrounded by walls of prestigious length. The walls of Igboho in northern Oyo are a good example. Many of the new towns founded under the stress of civil war were located in positions suitable for defence. They often lie beneath some rocky outcrop or a natural fortification.

A number of factors have been listed as being the causes for the fall of Oyo. One factor was, it is said, the ending of the slave trade by the British in the early 19th century. Although British decree did not stop the trade in slaves as such, it certainly made it more difficult; and this difficulty was reflected in economic disturbance. Too much emphasis may be placed on the significance of the slave trade. Perhaps more important is the fact that just as there were economic changes developing in the first years of the 19th century to the south of Oyo, so also were there political changes of enormous significance developing to the north; and it is possibly the northern rather than the southern stress that really precipitated the collapse of the Oyo empire. This northern stress was the rise of the Fulani as a result of the *jihad* of Uthman dan Fodio. The combination of pressure from the north and internal stresses brought an end to the Yoruba imperial structure which had existed in one form or another for at least three centuries. Moreover, it provided the circumstances that enabled the British from their base in Lagos to penetrate into the hinterland. By the end of the century virtually all the territory that had been under Oyo control had come under European colonial rule, either British or, in the case of Dahomey, French.

The collapse of the Oyo Empire and its successors has left a mark upon the Nigerian landscape which is still clearly visible in the shape of new towns and new patterns of settlement. Equally visible to the traveller are many signs of the other great force that dominated Nigerian 19th-century history, the rise of the Fulani Empire

Africa south of the Sahara during the course of the 19th century saw a number of Muslim *jihads* or holy wars. Some of the later *jihads* were provoked either directly or indirectly by the expansion of European colonial influence. The *jihad* of Uthman dan Fodio, formally proclaimed in 1804, is remarkable in that it was one of the very first of these movements and was apparently in no way provoked or concerned with the arrival of Western influence along the African coast. By the second decade of the 19th century the *jihad* of Uthman dan Fodio (he died in 1817) had united virtually the whole of northern Nigeria under one ruler. In the years that followed, while a segment of Borno managed to resist the Fulani advance, the states to the south were under constant threat of being incorporated into this new imperial structure. The Yoruba territory of Ilorin, at the junction between northern Yoruba country and northern Nigeria, rapidly came under Fulani influence. The state of Nupe fell to the Fulani expansion. By the middle of the century Fulani power had extended up the valley of the Benue into what is today the north of Cameroun, to create the Fulani feudatory state of Adamawa.

After Uthman dan Fodio's death the Fulani conquests were organized into what we now know as the Sokoto Caliphate. The resultant structure was extremely complex. On the one hand it consisted of a fairly decentralized system of emirates which were free to a very large extent to go their own way. On the other hand, all these emirates depended upon the prestige of the Caliph at Sokoto whose authority over them was as much religious as political. It is probably this Islamic theocratic element that gave the Sokoto Caliphate its enormous cohesion, despite the apparent decentralization of its component parts, and the great distances of some of the outlying regions such as Adamawa from the centre of Sokoto.

The history of modern Nigeria is inextricably bound up with the consequences of the *jihad* of Uthman dan Fodio. In the first place it gave a particular cohesion to the establishment of Islam in a large part of what was to become Nigeria. Secondly, the establishment of the Sokoto Caliphate, although the product of a great deal of conflict and conquest, undoubtedly resulted in an enormous increase in economic activity. Kano, for example, which travellers like Heinrich Barth visited in the middle of the 19th century, expanded significantly under the rule of the Sokoto Caliphate. Thirdly, the expansion of the Fulani disrupted the old pattern of pre-Islamic life. Many small groups of peoples were driven by the Jihadists into the mountains where some of them have survived to this day as isolated populations practising a way of life which has disappeared in those regions more accessible to Fulani attack. Some of the peoples who occupy the hills around the Jos plateau and the mountain tracks among the Mandara Mountains are examples of this phenomenon.

In the end the state created as a result of the *jihad* of Uthman dan Fodio attracted the attention of the colonial powers, the French, the British and in Cameroun the Germans, and by the end of the 19th century it was effectively squeezed between all three. In northern Cameroun the Germans acquired the extreme eastern part of the Fulani province of Adamawa. The French, expanding from the Niger bend, acquired what is today the territory of the Republic of Niger, which touched upon the area of the Hausa states that had formed the nucleus of the Fulani Empire. The bulk of the old Sokoto Caliphate finally came under British control in 1903. Instead of disappearing however, as had so many of the traditional states of Africa under the impact of colonialism, the Sokoto Caliphate survived because, through Lugard's policy of indirect rule, British influence was to a great extent exerted after 1903 through those very emirs whose origins lay in the *jihad* of Uthman dan Fodio. The result is that much of the old Sokoto Caliphate, its ceremonies, its traditions and its architecture can be seen to this day and, as some of the photographs in the pages that follow will make clear, this produces one of the most dramatic and fascinating aspects of the contemporary Nigerian scene.

The Islamic courts, with their traditional ceremonial, and the pattern of settlement among the Yoruba today, are but two of the aspects of Nigerian history which the observer of modern Nigeria can see for himself. Wherever you go among the reaches of the delta of the Niger, in the country of the Igbo, in the mountains along Nigeria's eastern border and on the edges of the Jos plateau, you can see in either pattern of settlement or way of life evidence of a complicated and sophisticated past. Much of this is not the matter of literary record but rather of the observation of what goes on today and evidence of what has gone on in the past. This kind of scene is, I believe, as well recorded by the camera of the traveller as it can be by the pen of the historian.

So this book has three separate aims. First to present Nigeria as she is today; as ever, in the process of change, but recorded at a single moment in time. Second, to make more people, both visitors who too often only see the cities, and Nigerians who may only know their own part of the country, aware of the extraordinary beauty, diversity and cohesion of Nigeria. And third, to salute a Great Nation on the 25th Anniversary of its Independence.

Overleaf: The Kogo Hills, near Kwoi, south Kaduna State

Below: Kukawa, the capital of Kanem-Borno, drawn by Heinrich Barth, 1851

THE LAND

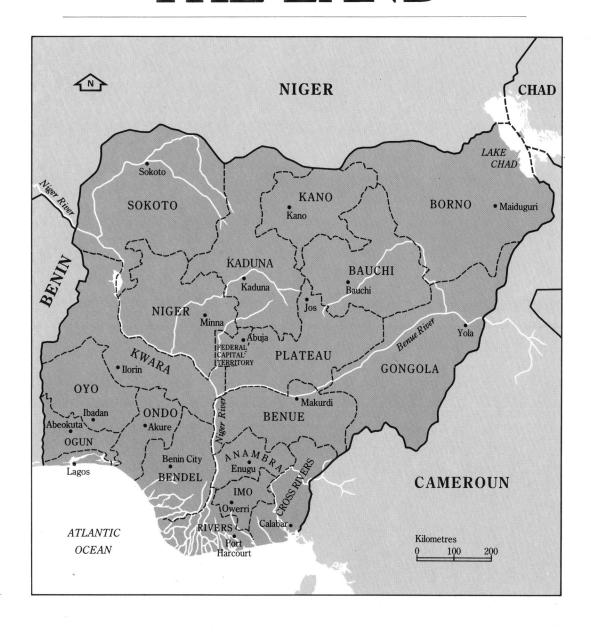

Nigeria is a vast country of many contrasts. In the far
south a sandbar protects the coast from the Atlantic
rollers.

Page 26: The rolling hills just
north of the river, Niger State

Above: Beach at the mouth of
New Calabar River, Rivers State

Opposite: Sandbars, Rivers State

Behind the coast are the swamps, the creeks and the forests of tropical Africa. Move northwards, and the forest becomes wooded plain and savannah, punctuated by massive granite inselbergs.

Left: Forest, Ondo State

Opposite: Village on remote creek, Bendel State

Overleaf
Page 32: Wooded plain, Oyo State

Page 33: The Zuma inselberg, Federal Capital Territory

In the centre there is a high cool plateau; and in the far north a fertile plain. Then the Sahara is approached.

Above: Looking north from an inselberg, Sokoto State

Opposite: The Hoss Valley, Plateau State

CHAPTER II

THE RIVERS

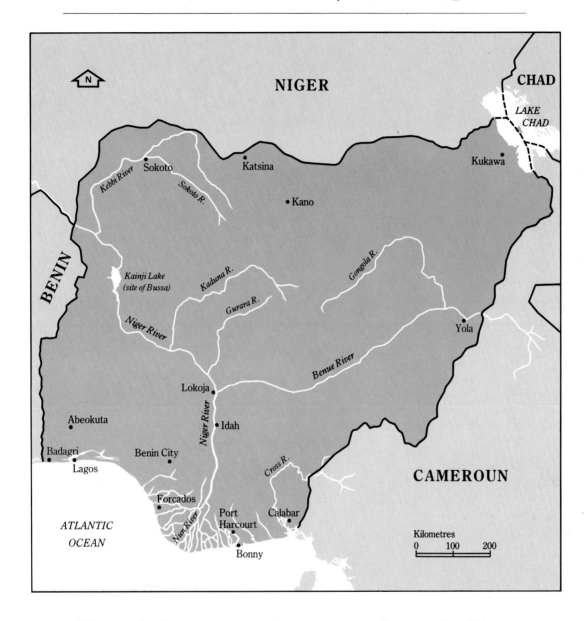

Through the country run two great rivers: the Niger and the Benue.

At Lokoja they meet, to continue southwards to the ocean.

Page 36: The Niger, well north of Kainji Dam

Above: The confluence of the Niger and Benue, as sketched by Captain William Allen RN in 1832–33

Opposite: The confluence today, with Lokoja, Kwara State

Nigerians have of course always known that the Niger
flowed southwards to the Atlantic. But in Europe the
course of the Niger caused a geographer's dispute which
lasted for centuries. It was in the search for the outlet of
this river that many 19th-century European travellers
made their reputations and sometimes lost their lives.

Preceding pages and above:
Lithographs from Captain William
Allen's *Picturesque Views of the
River Niger, sketched during
Lander's last visit in 1832–33*
Opposite: The Benue at Numan

Mungo Park died at Bussa, a place now deep under the
waters of the Kainji Dam. Hugh Clapperton passed this
way, eventually to die at Sokoto. Richard Lander and his
brother solved the mystery for Europe in 1830 when they
made their way down to the mouth of the Nun River,
thereby ending the dispute once and for all.

Above: Lithograph from the
drawing by Captain William Allen,
RN, 1832–3

Opposite: The Niger, where it
enters Kainji Lake

CHAPTER III

THE PEOPLE

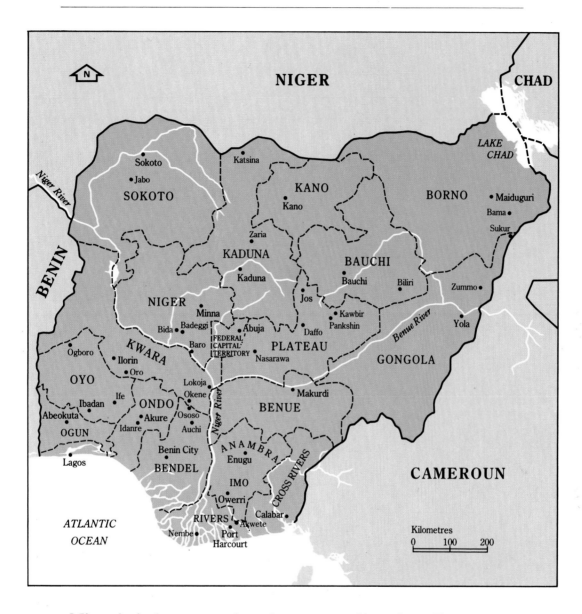

Nigeria is large not just because of its size. From the whole African continent one person in every four is a Nigerian. And the country's population is ever growing. The energy, the vivacity and the variety of its people seem endless.

Page 46: Emir's guard at Katsina
Sallah

Above: Family dressed in their
new Ide clothes, Zaria

Left: Oba of Ogboro on his throne, Oyo State

Below left: Idanre chief, Ondo State

Below right: Yoruba chief at the Oni of Ife's coronation, Oyo State

Above left: Yoruba taxi driver, Oro, Kwara State

Above right: Trader, Ososo, Bendel State

Left: Village elder, Kawbir, Plateau State

Opposite
Top left: Villager, Sukur, Gongola State

Top right: Fulani at Jabo market, Sokoto State

Bottom left: Villager, near Pankshin, Plateau State

Bottom right: Waja trader with distinctive tribal marks, Biliri market, Bauchi State

Opposite: Chiefs at turbaning ceremony, Bida

Left: Yoruba greetings during turbaning ceremony, Bida

Below: Chiefs in discussion, Nembe, Rivers State

Above left: Yoruba woman at ceremony, Ife

Above right: Woman near Jos

Left: Fulani woman at Yola

Opposite
Top left: Cloth seller at Okene, Kwara State

Top right: Igbira mother and child, Federal Capital Territory

Below left: Mother and child, Zummo, Gongola State

Below right: Laughing woman, Auchi, Bendel State

Overleaf:
Page 56: Rivers ladies dressed in Akwete cloth

Page 57: Woman with calabash, Bama, Borno State

Above left: Boy at Badeggi, Niger
State

Above right: Boy at Nasarawa,
Plateau State

Right: Girl at Bida

Opposite above: Boy with school
slate, Zaria

Opposite below: Girl at Lokoja,
Kwara State

Above left: Child in baby-tie on mother's back, Jabo, Sokoto State

Above right: Girl at Baro, Niger State

Left: Girl at Biliri, Bauchi State

Above left: Nupe boy, Bida

Above right: Fulani girl, Sokoto State

Right: Boy in Ide clothes, Zaria

Overleaf
Page 62: Girl selling oranges, Lokoja, Kwara State

Page 63: Boy herdsman, Daffo, Plateau State

CHAPTER IV

THE SOUTH WEST

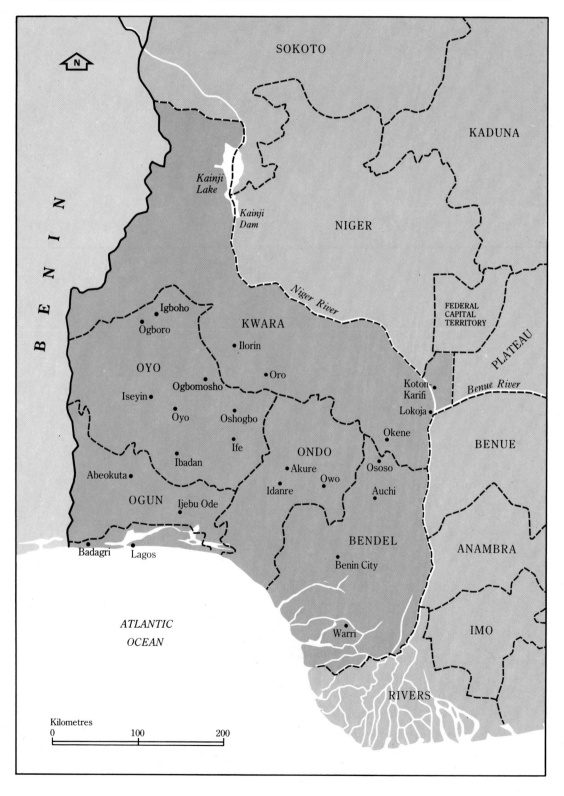

Lagos is the natural starting point for a tour of Nigeria,
which will take us through all nineteen states.

Lagos is an immense capital and harbour city, spreading across three islands and onto the mainland.

Page 64: Lagos harbour from the Federal Palace Hotel

Above: Lagos harbour

Opposite: Lagos from the air; the National Stadium in the middle distance

Above: View over Lagos,
Independence House prominent,
Victoria Island and the ocean
behind

Opposite: The new National
building, downtown Lagos

Behind Lagos is Ogun State. Here there are rivers and forests; the fishing and hunting can be excellent.

Abeokuta is the capital of Ogun State. There is a huge granite outcrop overlooking the city. Climb to its top and Abeokuta is spread out before you. The very word 'Abeokuta' means 'surrounded by rock', and in the caves people have surely sought refuge from time immemorial.

Above: Sasa River in Omo Forest Reserve, near Ijebu-Ode, Ogun State

Opposite: After a dawn shoot

Overleaf
Page 72: Looking up to the rocks above Abeokuta

Page 73: Abeokuta, the main mosque prominent

A great Yoruba Empire was once centred on what is today Oyo State. At Ife, ancestral home of the Yorubas, we may glimpse the ancient culture which must have been impressive indeed. The tradition of Ife as a centre of learning is carried on today by a splendid university.

Ibadan, one of the largest of all African cities, is the state capital. At Oshogbo the revival of the shrine of Oshun attracts thousands of pilgrims every year.

Above: The University of Ife campus

Above: Bronze head of a man, 12th–15th century AD, Ife

Overleaf
Page 76: Shrine at Oshogbo

Page 77 above: The city of Ibadan, seen from Cocoa House

Page 77 below: Night market at Iseyin

To the East lies Ondo State, rich in cocoa, scenery and history. Its southern border is the ocean, with fishing villages dotted along the creeks.

Above: A roadside vegetable stall, up-country Oyo

Opposite: Coastal fishing village, Ondo State

And where you least expect it, in the southern plains, you
find some of the grandest granite faces in all Nigeria.
These are the peaks of Idanre.

Above: The town of Idanre, set
amid granite

Opposite: Granite face at Idanre

Owo is famous both for its weaving and for the very fine terracottas that have been excavated there.

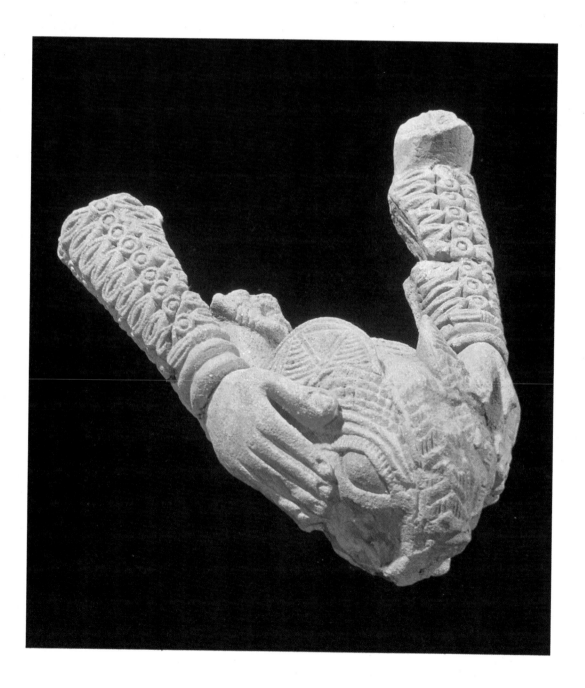

Above: Terracotta sculpture early
15th century AD, Owo

Opposite: Weaver of Owo

Bendel State stretches from the creeks and swamps bordering the ocean to the hills around Ososo.

Its history is rich, and its traditions are still maintained, as was seen during the coronation of the Oba of Benin in 1979.

The art of Benin is world-famous, and dates back some hundreds of years.

Above: Boatbuilding near Warri

Opposite: The hills of Ososo

Left: Dancers at Benin coronation

Below: Oba of Benin and Chiefs at his coronation

Above: Bronze equestrian figure,
probably 16th century AD, Benin

Kwara State, which stretches halfway across the country, from the western frontier to the confluence, has its own unique and rugged scenery. Ilorin, a city of tradition and history, is its capital.

Above: Waterfall on the Ore River

Opposite: Ilorin from the air

Preceding pages: Sunset near Lokoja

And there are several market towns such as Okene.

Opposite: Okene market

Below: Okene cloth seller

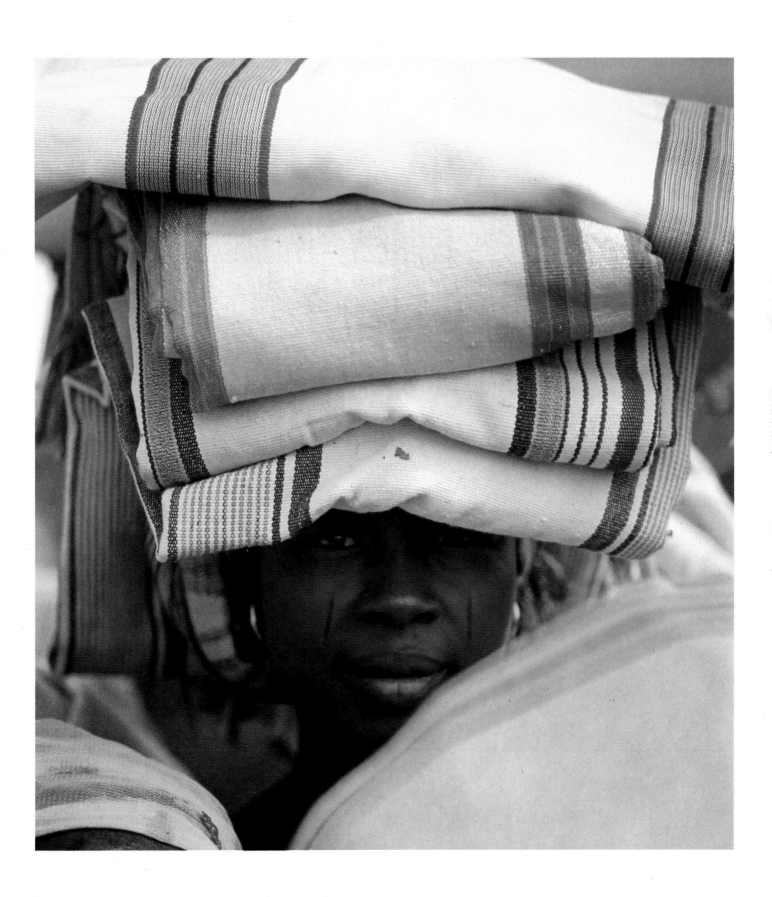

Opposite: The Niger above Koton-Karifi

Above left: The waterfront at Lokoja

Above right: Canoes at Koton-Karifi

Right: Canoe-making at Koton-Karifi

CHAPTER V
THE
NORTH WEST

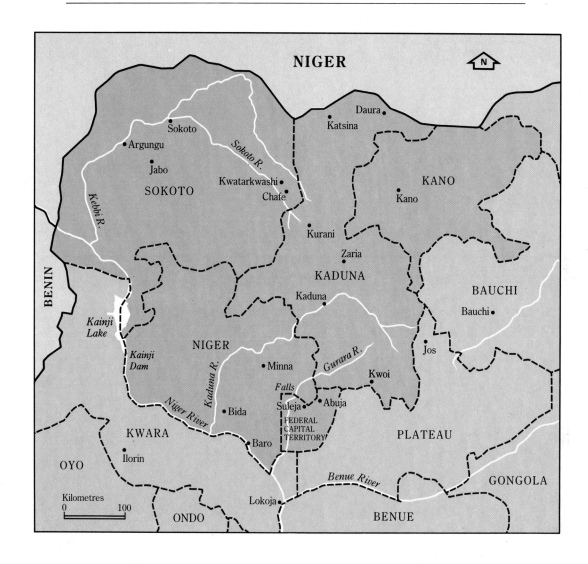

Just to the north of the Niger River lies Niger State. Many of its people are Nupes, founders of a very old civilization.

The ancient crafts of beadmaking, metalworking and weaving still flourish in Bida.

Page 96: Charge of the Emir's guards, Katsina Sallah

Opposite: The vegetable market, Bida

Left: Beadmaking, Bida
Below left: Cloth seller, Bida
Below right: Metalworking, Bida

And the ceremonial splendour of a turbaning continues.
Not far away are the thunderous Gurara falls.

Above: The Gurara Falls in flood

Opposite: Horsemen riding off in
parade, after the turbaning
ceremony at Bida

Sokoto State forms the north-west corner of Nigeria. This, too, was the centre of a great empire of the past. For over a century the Sultan of Sokoto ruled over an enormous territory. It was to here and to the rival empire of Borno that so many 19th-century travellers struggled in search of trade and geographical knowledge.

Above: Sokoto market, as seen by
Heinrich Barth in 1853

Today Sokoto is still famous, not least because of its colourful agricultural markets.

Many people gather for the annual fishing festival at Argungu.

Above: Agricultural market at Jabo

Overleaf: The fishing festival at Argungu

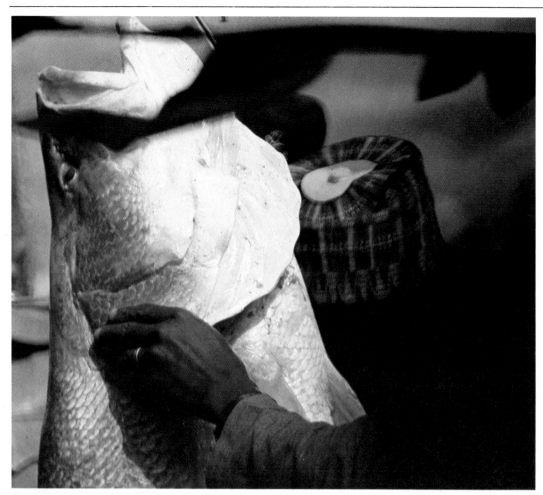

Left: Fish being weighed at
Argungu Fishing Festival

Below: Fishermen with butterfly
nets, Argungu

Above left: Hat seller, Chafe market

Above right: Calabashes for sale, Chafe market

Turning eastwards, we come to Kaduna State. Here there are ancient cities such as Zaria, with its fine architecture, both old and new.

Right: Part of the wall of the Emir of Zaria's palace

Below: Older buildings at Zaria

Opposite: An Ahmadu Bello University building, Zaria

Katsina was among the greatest of all Saharan market cities.

Its Sallah is renowned far and wide as a fascinating spectacle.

Right, below: The charge of salutation by the Emir's guards, Katsina Sallah

Opposite: The Emir of Katsina leaving the square at the end of the Sallah

Daura retains its aura of peace and dignity and is still
unspoiled.

THIS IS THE WELL AT WHICH, ACCORDING TO
ANCIENT LEGEND,

BAYAJIDA

THE SON OF THE KING OF BAGHDAD,
SLEW THE FETISH SNAKE KNOWN AS SARKI
AND AFTERWARDS MARRIED THE REIGNING

QUEEN OF DAURA.

THEIR SON, BAWO, BEGAT THE FIRST RULERS OF THE
SEVEN HAUSA STATES WHO WERE THE ORIGINS
OF THE HAUSA RACE.

Above: Plaque at the well of Daura

Opposite: A servant of the Emir of
Daura inspecting the wares of a
thread seller outside the palace

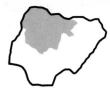

Above: Women pounding grain in the time-honoured way, Kwatarkwashi

Left: Brickmaking

Life in the country continues much as it has for decades,
hard-working and productive.

Above: The serene and beautiful
village of Kurani

Katsina and Kano were always bitter trading rivals; but in 1852, when Heinrich Barth reached Kano, it was the most important market city south of the Sahara. He has left us a splendid description of Kano as he found it. Although today the city is vastly larger, the traditional trades still flourish.

Above right: Indigo pits at Kano

Below left: Hats worn by the Hausa being stretched

Below right: Bead stall in Kano market

Opposite: Rigona stall in Kano market

BODY GUARD
OF THE SHEIKH OF BORNOU.

Published Feb. 1826. by John Murray, London.

CHAPTER VI
THE NORTH EAST

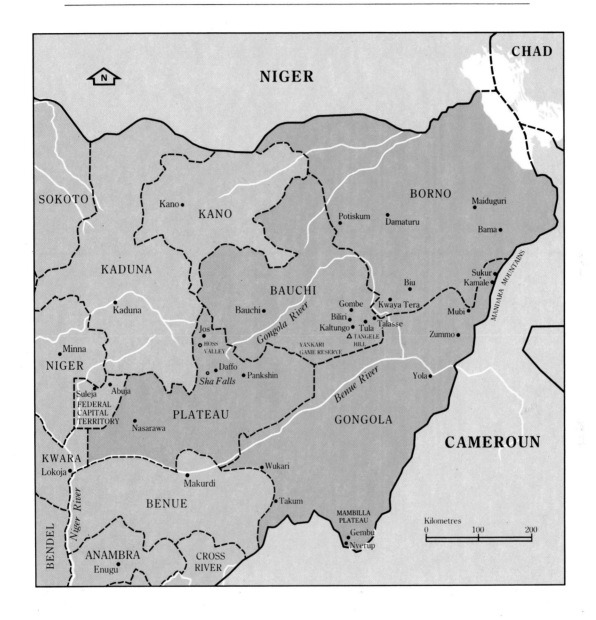

All over the north great baobab trees dot the plains as if
sleeping giants.

Borno, once the great rival of the Sokoto Empire, has a
distinct and ancient history of its own.

Page 118: Borno knight, drawn by
Captain Hugh Clapperton, 1823

Above: A baobab tree at dawn,
Borno

Opposite: Views of the Lake Chad
area, drawn by Heinrich Barth,
1851

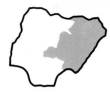

Even today Borno has an individual character, from the clothes and hair styles of the women to the language.

Above: The market at Potiskum

Top: Kanuri girls, near Bama

Above: A carved calabash of Borno

Right: Kanuri woman, near Damaturu

Bauchi State combines remote hills and rich agricultural land.

This page and opposite: Market scenes at Kwaya Tera

Towering over all is the hill of Tangale.

The hills of Tula, with their tough mountain people, are just to the north.

Below: Tangale Hill, from its northern base

Opposite: Hut and tree near Kaltungo

Overleaf
Page 128: Potter at Talasse

Page 129: Blind ropemaker at Tula

The game park at Yankari is a reserve for many of the
animals that once roamed Nigeria.

Above: Baboon

Right: Elephants

Plateau State, with its capital at Jos, is renowned for its cool invigorating climate. This was the environment in which one of Nigeria's earliest cultures, the Nok, flourished.

It is a land of secluded villages among the rocks, magnificent waterfalls and remote valleys.

Above: Nok terracotta head

Above: Grain storage huts, Nasarawa

Overleaf and following pages
Page 134 above: Village near Daffo

Page 134 below: Women pounding in a village south of Jos

Page 135: The Sha waterfall on the Farin Ruwa River, near Mama

Pages 136–7: The Hoss valley

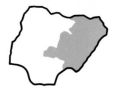

Gongola State lies along the border with Cameroun.

Here are high plateaux and extraordinary volcanic rock formations.

Right: The King of Sukur in his mountain fastness

Below: Kamale Pinnacle

Opposite: Mandara Mountains, looking down into Nigeria from the Cameroun plateau

The Mambilla plateau is difficult of access, but the journey
is well worthwhile, for here there are rolling highlands,
misty rivers and cool air.

Above: A typically sturdy hill
family of the Mambilla plateau,
near Nverup

Right: The northern edge of the
Mambilla plateau

Below: Early morning mist on the
Donga River, near Gembu

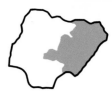

The finest of all Nigerian cloth is woven on the looms of
the Zummo area, north of Yola.

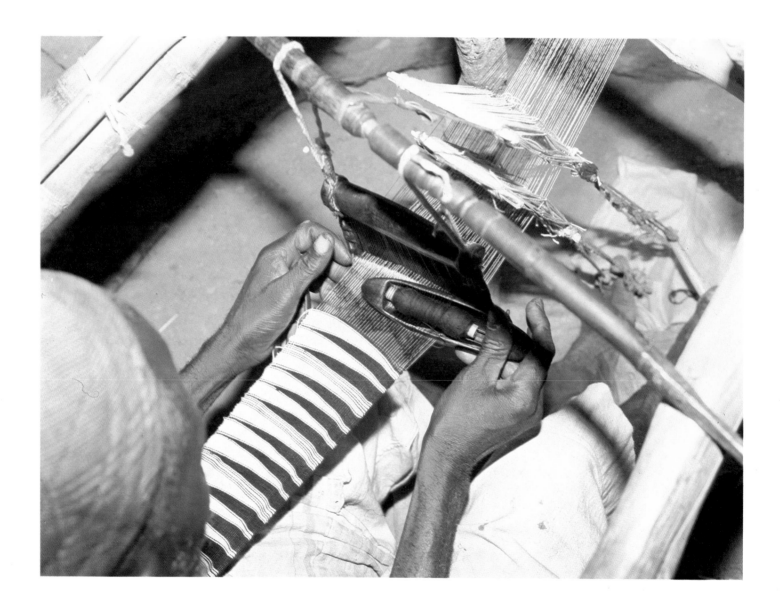

Above: Close-up of the man's
horizontal loom, near Zummo

Opposite: An example of this very
fine weaving. A narrow strip *tobe*,
or *rigona*, from Zummo

A familiar sight, as you travel through the North, is the
nomadic Fulani, ever on the move with their cattle. . .

Above: Fulani and cattle, near
Takum, Gongola State

. . . ever intriguing in their customs and dress.

Above: Fulani on the move, south
of Jos, Plateau State

Left: Fulani musician, near Bauchi

Below: Fulani mother and children

Opposite
Top left: Fulani woman at market, Yola

Top right: Fulani boy, Biliri

Below left: Jewellery on Fulani bridegroom

Below right: Fulani at market, Biliri

Overleaf:
Page 148: Fulani selling curd, Kwaya Tera

Page 149: Fulani woman at Bida market

THE
SOUTH EAST

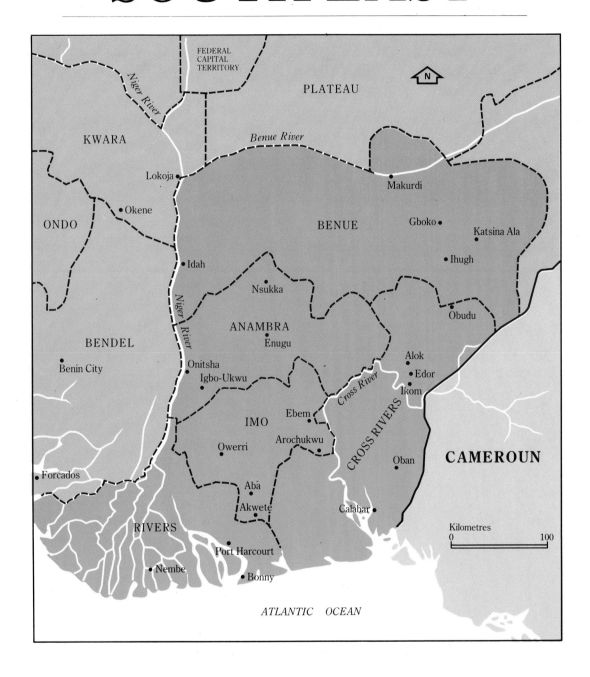

Benue State is a region of fishermen and farmers.

Page 150: The hills of Obudu

Above: Canoes at Idah

Opposite: The Niger near Idah

The Cliffs at Idah were often remarked on by the early travellers.

Above: Lithograph by Captain William Allen of the Cliffs at Idah, 1841

They remain an impressive landmark on the Niger today.

Above: The Cliffs at Idah today

Opposite: Tiv dressed in
traditional cloth at market, Ihugh

Below: Huts at sunset in the
harmattan season, Gboko

In Anambra rolling hills contrast with rich forest. Here is
the archaeological site of Igbo-Ukwu, which has yielded up
masterpieces of great interest; the renowned University
of Nsukka; and the main east–west artery of the country,
the bridge near the market city of Onitsha.

Opposite above: University of
Nsukka building

Opposite below: The bridge of
Onitsha

Above: Bronze pot and a stand,
roped together. Probably cast in
several pieces and brazed
together, Igbo-Ukwu, 9th
century AD

Imo State lies to the south.

At Arochukwu is the famous cave of the Oracle or Long Juju.

Below: Yam seedlings and cocoa, Ebem

Opposite: The cave of the Oracle or Long Juju at Arochukwu

Much of the country is covered by primary or secondary forest.

Above: Forest in south-eastern
Imo

Akwete is famous for its cloth, finely woven on the
woman's loom.

Above: Woman's loom, Akwete

In Cross River State, in the area just north of Ikom, there are some strange granite monoliths or Akwanshi, relics of an older culture.

Opposite: Monolith near Edor

Right: Monolith from the Nnam area, now at the National Museum, Lagos

Below: Monoliths in marketplace at Alok

Cross River State stretches from the mountains of Obudu in the north to the ocean in the south. With a heavy rainfall there is excellent agriculture.

Left: On the way to market, Obudu

Below: Bus on the Cross River

Opposite: Tea plantations in the hills near Oban

Bordering the ocean is Rivers State. This is a land of waterways and fishing. Ancient traditions and festivals are still observed.

Preceding pages: War canoes at a coronation, Nembe

Left: Chiefs at the same coronation

Below: Dancing to celebrate the accession of the new King of Nembe

Port Harcourt is the capital and main commercial centre of
Rivers State.

Because there are so many waterways, travel by boat is
often easier than by road.

Above: The act of coronation of
the Mingi or King of Nembe

Overleaf
Page 172: Hotel and golf course,
Port Harcourt

Page 173: Waterways, old seismic
lines and oilfields in Rivers State

NATURE

Nigeria is a naturalist's paradise.

Opposite above: Bitter gourd in light secondary forest, western Oyo State

Opposite below: Flower of African tulip tree on hilltop, Lokoja, Kwara State

Above: Dardanus swallowtail fluttering over clerodendrom flowers in a village garden, Akwete, Imo State

The bird life is extraordinarily rich.

Above: Bateleur near Biu, Borno State

Opposite
Above left: Fire-crowned bishop in Hoss Valley, Plateau State

Above right: Carmine bee-eater near Bama, Borno State

Below: Pin-tailed whydah near Yola, Gongola State

Indeed all forms of wildlife are there to be studied.

Left: Female golden orb weaver spider, Anambra State

Below: Variegated grasshopper, Zaria, Kaduna State

Opposite: Angola white lady swallowtails mating, Benue State

Above left: Termite hills near
Kainji, Kwara State

Above right: Monkey jumping,
Lokoja, Kwara State

Opposite
Above: African beauty snake near
Gombe, Bauchi State
Below: Forest cobra near Kwoi,
Kaduna State

CHAPTER IX

AGRICULTURE AND DEVELOPMENT

Not too long ago Nigeria was a major exporter of many agricultural products. Today, because of a larger population, high expectations and a drift to the cities, Nigeria is a net importer. The authorities realize the urgency of the situation. What is planned is a policy of making agriculture more attractive together with mechanization of farming methods. Given success, Nigeria could once again approach self-sufficiency and be a net exporter of some cash crops. The future is indeed in agriculture.

Page 182: Agricultural experts at an experimental farm, examining improved strains of cassava, Rivers State

Page 183: The old – working the hard way

Page 183: The new – mechanized tobacco seedling planting

Left: Collecting rubber latex from trees. Cross River State

Below: Raw cotton ready for shipment to the gin, near Danbarta, Kano State

Opposite
Top left: Tobacco drying, Bendel State

Top right: Corn, stored safely out of the reach of rodents, Plateau State

Below left: Palm oil kernels, Rivers State

Below right: Groundnuts in a Sokoto market

The search for oil began in the 1930s, but it was 20 years
before success was achieved in the late '50s. The oilfields
are spread over some of the most difficult terrain in the
Delta. There are sufficient reserves of oil and gas to
ensure that Nigeria will be a major producer of
hydrocarbons well into the next century.

Above: A swamp rig at work,
Bendel State

Opposite: Pipelaying in Rivers
State

The income from crude oil exports has allowed an ambitious development of the infrastructure of the country.

Above: Kainji Dam, Kwara State

Opposite: The bridge over the river Niger at Koton-Karifi, Kwara State

Roads and harbours in particular have been developed with
speed and flair.

Above: Road building near Ososo,
Bendel State

Opposite: The impressive complex
of Lagos harbour

Nigeria is blessed with a young and virile population. It possesses abundant natural resources. Given wise channelling of all this energy, the future of Nigeria is bright indeed.

NOTES ON PHOTOGRAPHS

1,5 See notes 98–99, 101.

2 Butterfly fishing nets (homa, or clap nets) in use on the Sokoto River. See also 104–106.

6 See notes 66–69 on Lagos.
8–9 See notes 36, 40–45 on the Niger River.
10 See notes 126–127.
12 (above) See notes 116–117 (below) See notes 138–139.
23 See note 123.

24–25 The granite Kogo hills, some 16 km west of Kwoi, are easily accessible from the Federal Capital-to-be at Abuja, and offer some splendid walking. Some of the inselbergs require rock-climbing to reach their summits, but the granite is rough and the angle seldom extreme.

28 The superb beach at the mouth of the New Calabar River is 2 km long and 100–300 m wide. It is uninhabited except for a solitary fisherman's hut, only occasionally occupied. It backs on to swamp and can therefore only be reached by boat, an undertaking that is somewhat hazardous at high tide but perfectly simple at middle or low water.

29 Offshore sandbars are seldom accessible and are often submerged at high tide. Like the river sandbars, they are continually shifting, as the literature of the 18th- and 19th-century navigators shows. Here we see the very first stage in the many tens of millions of years of the oil-forming process in the Niger Delta. The remains of dead marine organisms, if conditions are favourable, continually get covered by sand, clay and eventually rock. With pressure and heat and time these organisms may become metamorphosed into oil and gas, and diffuse through rock layers, and collect in sand bodies like these bars.

30 Most early travellers recorded their aversion to the mangrove swamps of the Delta. Thus in 1837 one wrote of 'an indescribable feeling of heaviness (and) languor . . . which requires a considerable effort to shake off'. While their comments may in part have been coloured by the fearful toll that malaria inflicted, the swamps even today are uneasy places to live. There is very little land, so the population remains thinly spread. Fishing is the main means of livelihood. Standards of living for the most part remain low. Without the waterways through the mangrove, whether river or creek, passage would be impossible; and even with them, communications are often difficult and tortuous.

31 The tropical forest is a place of wonder. Strange noises and even stranger silences beset you here. The main concern is that so many forests have been and are being felled for timber, and not replanted. Unless there is a real effort to replace what is harvested, Nigeria's forests will have largely disappeared by the end of this century.

32 (64, 77 below) A pleasant and interesting three-day trip can be had by following the old route to the north through western Oyo, tracing where possible the footsteps of 19th-century travellers such as Clapperton, Lander and Clarke.

The country to the west and north of Iseyin (where there is a splendid night market) is strikingly beautiful; and the sites of the old fortified hill-top towns (examples are Old Awaiye on Ado Rock, Irawo-ile, Shaki and, most impressive of all, Ogboro) make the journey especially worthwhile.

Pre-reading for such a journey should include Clapperton, Lander (both), Bowen, Clarke; for details see the Bibliography, page 207. And also Boscom, 'Lander's Routes through Yoruba Country' (*Nigerian Field* 25–1) and Gleave, 'Hill Settlements and their Abandonment in Western Yorubaland' (*Africa* XXII No. 4).

33 The granite hills or inselbergs of Nigeria remain something of a geological mystery. Various theories have been advanced as to their origin. It may be that they are the last remnant of vaster granite bodies that have almost eroded away. In times past they have provided refuge for harassed villagers from marauding warriors. Today they provide the rock climber with some excellent sport.

When on an inselberg watch for the hyrax, a nimble climber indeed, and also for monkeys and sometimes baboon. And on the rocks you may find indentations worn down by centuries of grinding of cereals.

34 The plateau, with Jos as a base, provides an excellent area for exploration, hill walking and picnicking. A month would not be sufficient to exhaust all the local possibilities. Hills, hidden valleys, waterfalls, lakes, rolling plateaux and abrupt precipices: the variety is enormous. The terrain caters for both the hardened trekker and the small toddler. For much of the year the air is clear, dry and invigorating; a considerable contrast to the more humid lowlands of the south.

35 Although much of the far north is flat, it too springs its surprises. Here the huge complex of the inselbergs at Kwatarkwashi provides a playground for hill walking or rock climbing. To the south lies a fertile agricultural plain; to the north often dessicated open country hints at the Sahara. For details of Kwatarkwashi inselbergs, see Zaria Field Society's *Guide*, page 82.

36, 40–45 The story of the European exploration of the Niger is fascinating. The late 18th-century maps of Africa still showed vast blanks over most of the interior of the continent. Little new had been learned since the 16th-century writings of Leo Africanus.

'The course of the Niger, the place of its rise and termination, and even its existence as a separate stream, are still undetermined', was a late-18th-century lament. With the delta a myriad of narrow channels or broader bodies of water that ended abruptly, there seemed little chance that the Niger flowed southwards into the Bight of Benin. More fashionable views among the leading geographers of the age were that it joined the Nile; or that it flowed under the Sahara to reach the Mediterranean; or that it flowed into the desert and simply evaporated.

In 1788 the African Association was founded in London 'for promoting the discovery of the interior part of Africa'. After several early failures by others, a young Scottish doctor, Mungo Park, reached the Niger in 1786 and ascertained that it flowed eastwards, and not westwards as many had thought. A second expedition by Park, in 1805, ended in disaster with the death of all its 44 Europeans. Park himself died in the rapids at Bussa, now deep under the waters of the Kainji Dam.

Further failures followed. Then in 1822 Walter Oudney, Hugh Clapperton and Dixon Denham, coming across the Sahara, reached Lake Chad, Kano and Sokoto. Oudney died, but the expedition was an undoubted success, the first to reach West Africa by the Saharan route. Clapperton and his servant Richard Lander returned to Sokoto a few years later, travelling up from Badagri on the coast. But Clapperton and most of his companions died, only young Richard Lander surviving. The mystery of where the Niger flowed remained as obscure as ever to Europeans.

Richard Lander and his brother John returned to the Niger and, starting from Bussa where Mungo Park had died, succeeded in reaching the ocean in 1830.

The second stage of the exploration of the Niger was the attempt to open it up to seaborne commerce. But the disastrous expedition of MacGregor Laird in 1832–4, when 37 of the party of 48 died, was a severe setback. Richard Lander himself died of a wound on this expedition at the age of 30.

Nearly a decade passed before the major expedition of 1841, lavishly financed by the British government, set sail. Replete with commissioners, chaplains, farmers and a bevy of scientists, the exploration was ambitious indeed. Once again malaria took its toll, and the expedition eventually ended in failure and retreat. Perhaps the most noteworthy participant was Samuel Crowther, a former Yoruba slave whose freedom had been bought some time before. Educated in Liverpool, he had become the first African clergyman of modern times. He eventually became the first Bishop of the Niger.

An answer to the problem of malaria came in with William Baikie's expedition of 1852. Although the prophylactic and healing qualities of cinchona bark and its extract quinine were recognized as early as the 17th century by the Jesuits, who gave it to their missionaries, it had not been generally accepted. It became known as 'Jesuit's bark' and the English, as good Protestants, wanted nothing to do with it. Baikie's crew took quinine and survived to a man. The way was clear for the opening up of the Niger Basin.

The summarized story of the exploration of the Niger and Benue can best be read in Bovill and de Gramont. The literature of the explorers is rich indeed, and much of it is in print today. See Bibliography, page 207.

38 and 39 The early explorers found no settlement at the confluence of the Niger and the Benue; there was plenty of better land elsewhere. The first attempt at establishing a model farm by the British was made during the 1841 expedition; it failed, however, within a few months.

Baikie settled there in 1859, and remained for five years. He built up Lokoja market with the help of the powerful Emir of Nupe, who befriended him. 'It was unlike any other African market in that it was closed on Sundays and bought slaves instead of selling them.' Once established, Lokoja's strategic trading situation ensured that the market would succeed. The now abandoned sheds of the famous trading houses still line the waterfront.

Today Lokoja is well worth visiting. At low water the riverside yam market is extensive. The Niger rises fully 10 m, however, so much of the market disappears with the coming of high water during the rains. Water buses of all kinds call at Lokoja.

And if you wish to view the confluence, drive up the hill behind the town for a magnificent view.

46–63 Nigerians are infinitely diverse. In appearance (contrast the short stocky Tiv with the very tall men of the Kalabaris) and in tradition (almost as various as the tribal structure), the lack of uniformity is everywhere. There are over 200 tribes and recorded languages. English is the only lingua franca, although Hausa is spoken in perhaps half the country. There are three major tribal groups: the Yorubas in the south west, the Igbos in the south east and the Hausa Fulani of the north. The minority tribes together, however, come close in number to these three major groups combined, and many of them have left their mark on history and are rightly proud of their heritage.

What is common to most Nigerians is their energy, vivacity and hospitality; and their fondness of children. No collection of photographs can truly reflect the Nigerian people; these may hint at the variety.

66–69 Lagos City spreads across three islands and onto the mainland. The islands are Lagos Island, which consists mainly of Government offices and a business sector; Ikoyi, now separated by only a few feet from Lagos, mainly a residential area, although some Government offices have recently been built on it; and across Five Cowrie Creek (named from the old ferry fare) Victoria Island, also mainly residential.

Lagos was of relatively minor importance until the 19th century, partly because access to its harbour was across a very difficult sandbar. Rivers further east provided better access to the ocean traders. Lagos acquired ever-increasing importance from 1850 onwards, although it was not until the construction of the two great moles in the second decade of this century that entry became easier. Today, in 1985, Lagos is the first city of Nigeria, and its Federal Capital.

70 Sport fishing is available in every state in Nigeria in one form or another. While offshore fishing in a boat can be exciting, the rivers provide a great variety of fishing. Most of the fish are edible. River fishing can vary from spinning on the upper reaches of the rivers that rise in the hills of Oyo and Ogon in the west, to deep stream fishing for the huge bass of the Benue and Niger. The keen itinerant fisherman could need quite a variety of equipment; but a medium-sized rod with a variety of lines and spinners will enable him to meet most situations.

71 Also good is the shooting. Firearms are very strictly controlled, however, so the authorities should be closely consulted. Shooting is forbidden in forest reserves and animal parks.

72–73 Abeokuta, which means 'surrounded by rock', was probably raised from the status of a village in the early 19th century. During the Yoruba civil wars of this period the Egba (a branch of the Yoruba) was attacked by armies from Ife and Ijebu-Ode. Compelled to retreat in a south-westerly direction, they found sanctuary in about 1830 among the rocks of Abeokuta. The Egba are keen traders, and as a result considerable wealth has been built up in Abeokuta.

Numerous guides will offer to show you the way to the top of the rock. It is best to pick one, so the others desist; the climb is not long or difficult, but rubber-soled shoes are essential and a modicum of agility is useful.

74–75 Ife, or Ile Ife to give it its proper name, is acknowledged by all Yoruba groups as their ancestral home. Very little is known of its early history. It seems probable that at some time during the first millennium AD strangers from the north east either invaded or settled at Ife, establishing a kingdom there. As Crowther has written:

> The Yoruba creation myth that probably parallels this event talks of Ile Ife as the origin of life. In the beginning the earth was covered with water. Olorun, the supreme god, let his son Oduduwa down a chain carrying a handful of earth, a cockerel and a palm nut. Oduduwa scattered the earth over the water and the cockerel scratched it so that it became the land on which the palm tree grew. Its sixteen branches represented the sixteen crowned heads of Yorubaland, probably the heads of the main settlements established by the newcomers.

The origins of the art of Ife are enigmatic. Preliminary datings suggest the 12th–15th centuries as being the period of greatest activity. But beyond the beauty and sophistication of the bronze heads in particular, not a great deal is known for certain. For details see Ekpo Eyo, *Two Thousand Years of Nigerian Art*.

76 Oshogbo is not more than three centuries old. It is the site of the great battle between the Fulani invaders from the north and the Yoruba armies of the south in 1838–9. The Fulani were decisively defeated in

the forests around Oshogbo, where their cavalry was hemmed in, and Oshogbo marks the furthest point of their advance south. Legend gives much credit for the defeat of the Fulani to the goddess Oshun, who resides in the river near Oshogbo. In recent years there has been a revival of her cult, and in the numbers making the pilgrimage to Oshogbo. For details, see Ulli Beier, *The Return of the Gods* and S. Johnson, *The History of the Yorubas*.

77 above Ibadan, today one of Africa's most populous cities, is of very recent origin. It was founded in a great wood among seven hills by a mixed group of Yoruba soldiery who made their base there in the 1850s, during the troubles caused by the Yoruba civil wars and the Fulani attacks. It attracted refugees and armed bands from a wide area, and eventually its army became the most powerful in Yorubaland.

Ibadan is one of the great markets of Nigeria. Today its inhabitants are estimated to number several million.

77 below See note 32.

79 The coastal villages of Ondo State, cut off as they are from the mainland by swamps and creeks, are extremely remote. Many of the houses are on stilts, and for some of the villagers dry land must be a rare sight. The main livelihood is fishing.

80–81 The rocks of Idanre are a magnificent place for the naturalist, the walker or the climber. The best approach is up the long rock pathway to the village of Old Idanre on the crest above the modern town. From here there are splendid day-long walks and scrambles across the tops of the granite hills.

82 There are two very distinct types of indigenous weaving in Nigeria: the man's narrow strip hand loom (see 142–143) which is common over much of West Africa, albeit with many local variations; and the woman's vertical loom, pictured here, which can be found only in Nigeria and parts of Cameroun. Owo was once an important centre of the woman's loom. For further details see Lamb and Holmes, *Nigerian Weaving*.

83 The people of Owo, the capital of Ondo State, are said to have migrated from Ile Ife, the ancestral home of all Yorubas, in about the 12th century AD. By the 15th century Owo was part of the mighty Benin empire (see 86–87); at roughly the same time the craftsmen of Owo were reaching their height of creativity. One result was a series of splendid terracottas.

85 Ososo town is notable mainly for its situation, high up in the granite hills south of Okene. Many of its houses are built on or among the rocks. It used to be very difficult to reach, but with new roads this is no longer the case. The people, Edos, who long ago emigrated northwards from Benin, reflect their former isolation with a robust independence. The scenery is superb in this area, and many worthwhile excursions can be made in the region of Ososo.

86–87 The history of Benin is rich indeed. The city dates back about a thousand years, and is the focal point of the Edo-speaking people. It

was one of the early and great empires of West Africa. During the 15th century the Benin Empire spread from the River Niger in the east to what was Dahomey and is now the Republic of Benin in the west; and well into the hills of the Yoruba Ekiti to the north. Benin city, with its complex system of defensive walls, its large army, its hierarchy of chiefs, its elaborate court ceremonial, and above all its highly developed art, both secular and sacred, was probably based on considerable trade with the Hausa North. The Oba or King of Benin is one of the more important hereditary rulers. His court maintains many of its traditional ceremonies, as was seen during his elaborate coronation in 1979.

The best-known African sculptures in bronze come from Benin city. The Oba or King had a monopoly of the work, and maintained specialist guilds of bronzesmiths, wood and ivory carvers and beadmakers. This was court art *par excellence*, and bronzesmiths were executed for working for anyone outside the court. Some 90% of Benin art was carried out in bronze, and the craftsmanship reached superb levels.

For details of Benin's history and art, see especially Ekpo Eyo, *Two Thousand Years of Nigerian Art*, Alan Ryder, *Benin and the Europeans 1485–1897*, Jacob Egharevba, *A Short History of Benin*, and R.E. Bradbury, *the Benin Kingdom*.

88–89 Sunset a few kilometres to the west of Lokoja, looking towards the hills on the Kebba road. The countryside in the triangle Okene–Kebba–Lokoja is relatively uninhabited, whether from shortage of water or the disturbances of the mid-19th century it is difficult to say.

90 The Ore waterfall near Oke-Oyan is a fine half-day outing from Ilorin. Drive on the main Ilorin–Kebba road as far as Omu-Aran, then turn northwards on a good laterite road for some 30 km. The turning to the village is signposted. Leaving your car, engage a guide and begin the 40-minute walk to the falls. These drop abruptly from the plateau above, with a clear 30 m fall. There is a fine pool at their base to cool off in.

91 'Ilorin' means 'home of elephants'. The city is said to have been founded by Yoruba hunters only a few centuries ago. The Fulani invaders from the north took the city in 1831, when it became an emirate. Although the first Emir is said to have 'subdued all Yoruba proper', Ilorin was the southernmost city held by the Fulani; it is still strongly Muslim today. The great new mosque is clearly visible in the centre of the city.

92–93 Okene is one of the main centres of the Igbira people, an industrious people renowned for their farming abilities who are centred on a thriving town. Okene market takes place every other day. It is well worth visiting. The town is built over several rocky hills, which lend scale and grandeur to the site. Of particular interest in the market is the large cloth section, and buyers come from far afield to purchase the famous Okene cloths.

95 Koton-Karifi is 33 km north of the confluence, on the Niger. It is the site of a magnificent new bridge (see page 189). Many of the inhabitants are adroit fishermen, for the multiple streams of the Niger teem with fish. (For Lokoja see pages 38–39 and notes thereon.)

96 See notes 110–111.

98-99, 101 Bida is today the main town of the Nupe people. Up to the 15th century this area, just to the north of the Niger River and around the Kaduna River, was subject to the Ata or King of Idah. Legend has it that a son of this king by a Nupe woman established the Nupe kingdom and became the first Etsu Nupe or King of it. The kingdom reached its height of power in the second half of the 18th century. It was rent by civil war in the first half of the 19th century; eventually a Fulani preacher, Mallam Deno, won power. His son moved the capital of the Nupe kingdom to Bida in 1850.

Bida is renowned as a centre for many crafts. The weavers and embroiderers, brass- and silversmiths, beadmakers, tailors and leatherworkers are all famous for their skills. Indeed, Bida probably has a greater concentration of these crafts than any other single place in Nigeria.

Traditional title holders are invested in their office in a ceremony that includes placing a turban on the head. Hence the ceremony is known as

'turbaning'; it is followed by a grand parade of the Niger nobility on horseback.

100 The Gurara Falls are a raging torrent in the rainy season (June–September), although at the height of the dry season they are reduced to a trickle of water. Situated at 9°19′N, 7°01′E, they are found by driving for some 3 km down a dirt track to the east of the main Minna to Suleja road; the turning off the main road is some 78 km from Minna or 32 km from Suleja.

102 Sokoto was established by Uthman dan Fodio's son Muhammad Bello in 1809 (see also note 144–149); so it is of relatively recent foundation. Clapperton visited Bello in 1824 and died at Sokoto in 1826. Barth passed through Sokoto in 1853, and received a very hospitable welcome.

The Sultan of Sokoto is still, as dan Fodio was, Sarkin Musulmi, or Commander of the Faithful (see note 144–149). Today this is a spiritual title, and can best be translated as spiritual leader of all Muslims in Nigeria.

Sokoto, after declining somewhat in importance in the second half of the last century, is once again expanding rapidly and has become a major city. The market, which Barth describes, is best seen on a Friday.

104–106 The butterfly fishing nets (homa, or clap nets) of Sokoto are beautiful to watch in use. And once a year, at Argungu, there is a fishing festival in a specially stocked branch of the Sokoto River where enormous fish (giwan ruwa) of over 50 kg are caught in these simple handnets.

108–109 Zaria is one of the seven 'legitimate' Hausa states (see note 112–113 on Daura). There was human settlement on or below the two inselbergs near the city from early times, for many Stone Age implements have been found there. By the 15th century AD the town had walls, and had become the capital of the Zegzeg Empire. The famous warrior Queen Amina reigned in the early 16th century. The Kano Chronicle says 'at this time Zaria, under Queen Amina, conquered all the towns as far as Kwararafa and Nupe. Every town paid tribute to her.'

96, 110–111 The two great Muslim festivals, Ide el Fitr (which celebrates the ending of the holy month of Ramadan) and Ide el Kabir (which commemorates Abraham sacrificing a ram instead of his son Isaac), are both marked in the northern Emirates by a Sallah. The Sallah of Katsina is a magnificent spectacle.

The day begins with prayers outside the town. Then there is a parade from the prayer ground to the public square before the Emir's palace. Each district or village group march to their appointed place on the square. Last of all the Emir and his entourage arrive. He takes his place before the palace to receive the *jahi*, or salutation, of the horsemen. Those on foot retire and the riders gallop the length of the square, before pulling up abruptly before the Emir to salute him with a raised right fist. Each district's cavalry gallops up in turn; last, and most fierce, are the Emir's bodyguard. Then silence descends as the Emir gives an address. The noise, the splendour, the colour are superb.

112–113 Daura is still unspoiled today and well worth visiting. It is famous as the place where the legendary hero Bayajidda, son of the King of Baghdad, killed the evil snake, married the Queen and had seven sons. These were the founders of the seven 'legitimate' Hausa states: Daura, Kano, Katsina, Zaria, Biram, Rano and Gobir.

116–117 Kano is a very old city. Fortified as an agricultural centre in the distant past, with the Dalla Hill as a superstitious centre, by 1400 it had emerged as one of the three most important city states in the region (the others being Zaria and Katsina). In 1526 Leo Africanus wrote of Kano:

> The inhabitants are rich merchants and most civil people. Their King was in times past of great puissance, and he had mighty troops of horsemen at his command, but he has since been constrained to pay tribute to the Kings of Zaria and Katsina.

There was continuing rivalry between Katsina and Kano in particular as to which city should be the great southern entrepôt for the Saharan trade. After the *jihad* of dan Fodio in the first decade of the 19th century, Katsina declined and Kano prospered.

Barth, perhaps the greatest of all the 19th-century Saharan travellers, has left us a splendid description of Kano in 1851:

> The market is generally immensely crowded during the heat of the day, and offers a most interesting scene . . . The principal commerce of Kano consists in native produce, namely, the cotton cloth woven and dyed here . . . in the form of tobes or rigona . . . There is really something grand in this kind of industry, which spreads to the north as far as Murzuk, Ghat and even Tripoli. . .

Moreover:

> beads, in very great variety, form an important article of import.

The city has grown enormously. However, Kano's old market remains much as it was in Barth's day, and it is still the main entrepôt for trading in the north.

120 'The Baobab tree, *Adansonia digitata*, is perhaps the best known of all African trees. It is often planted around villages because it is a very useful tree. The young leaves are cooked and eaten as a spinach, the pulp around the seeds inside the hard fruit is eaten (a fruity, slightly acidic flavour), and the bark is stripped off to make a fibrous twine. The large white flowers on the Baobab tree last only for a single day.' (*Zaria Field Society Guide*) And, of course, it produces that most valuable African commodity, shade.

123 The people of Borno, the Kanuri, are very different from the Hausa or the Fulani of north-west and north-central Nigeria. They speak a Nilo-Saharan language which bears no relation to Hausa, and their history is very distinct.

Of all the areas of Nigeria, Borno has the longest continually known history. the Kanem-Borno Empire, based on the Chad basin, was already a major force by the year AD 1000. By the 14th century the Empire was declining, and around 1390 the Mai or King withdrew to the western shores of Lake Chad, today's Borno. By the beginning of the 17th century the Borno Empire was well established once again and was the most powerful state in western and central Sudan. It was strong enough to withstand the Fulani *jihad* (holy war) of the early 19th century, thanks to the inspired leadership of one from another cattle-owning nomadic people, the Kanembu, who came from the old kingdom of Kanem. Al-Kanemi eventually replaced the Mai of Borno in all but name. As Clapperton, who visited Borno in 1821, wrote:

the Sultan-ship of Borno is but a name; the court still keeps up considerable state, and adheres strictly to its ancient customs, and this is the privilege left them.

Clapperton and Denham were most impressed by the effective ruler of Borno, Al-Kanemi. In 1846 the Mai led a revolt against Al-Kanemi's son; the revolt was crushed and the Mai executed. This ended one of the longest and most celebrated dynasties in African history.

Today Borno still retains its individual flavour. The layout of the villages, the language, the clothing and hair style of the women, all point to the distinct character of the Kanuri people.

126–127 The area south of Gombe in Bauchi State is a superb area for hill walking and exploration on foot.

The ascent of Tangale Hill is a long dry climb and takes 2½–3 hours from its base. The permission of the Emir of Kaltungo should be sought. With his consent one of the local hunters can be hired as a guide, which is necessary as the route is tortuous. From the eastern base of the mountain, the first stage is up winding paths to a leafy shoulder. Then a steep and tiring earth and stone slope leads to rock. There is a path which can only be found and kept to with difficulty, so full of zigzags is it; but there are no technical difficulties whatsoever if the path is followed.

Tangale Hill is a tertiary volcanic core. To the north is one of the few good fossil beds in the country; these contain Cretaceous ammonites which can be found in the stream bed (when it is dry) near Pindiga.

To the south lies an immense eroded anticline of tertiary age, running east–west. It is some 50 km long and 5 to 10 km wide. There are no roads into this immense Didiya Hills sanctuary, which is sparsely inhabited by Fulani. The easiest way to walk in is by the inlet of the Bolleri river which cuts through the hills of the northern flank 7 km

south of Bambam. This northern entrance descends a sequence of huge granite steps, so the approach is on foot; once through the gorge there is a convenient isolated hill to climb to view the centre of the sanctuary. At least 2½ hours should be allowed from the entrance to the top of the isolated hill and back.

The Tangale tribe, from which Tangale Peak derives its name, are a tough mountain people who were mentioned in the books of the early administrators as being fierce warriors; today they still retain a sturdy independence in their attitudes.

128–129 Journey to Tula (and Wala Waja). A very worthwhile half-day expedition leaves the main Gombe–Numan road at the signpost for Tula and takes a dirt road up over the hills. Tula is reached after 15 km and it must be one of the most beautiful villages in the whole of Nigeria, set as it is on two levels of rock terraces and with extraordinary rock formations. The agricultural terracing is also extremely impressive.

If time is short a visit to Tula and Tula Baule, another 4 km along the road, allows you to see the highlights of this excursion. If a half day is available and it is the dry season, a round trip can be made through Wala Waja and back to Gombe.

130–131 The Yankari Game Reserve lies to the south east of Bauchi, about 100 km by road. There is an encampment of modern and comfortable huts for the traveller. Below the hotel complex is a delightful warm spring where excellent bathing under huge trees can be had; beware of the baboons, who delight in snatching towels and clothing left unattended and pelting swimmers with sticks.

132 During the late Stone Age, perhaps between 500 BC and AD 200, a vigorous culture existed across much of what is Plateau State today. The first evidence of this culture was discovered in 1936 in the shape of a terracotta head of a monkey; since then many more finds have confirmed its existence. The Nok people were agriculturalists and probably kept cattle. They knew how to smelt iron, a skill they may have acquired from Egypt via Carthage and the trans-Saharan trade routes. They were fond of jewellery, for many of their terracotta figures wear necklaces and bracelets. Some of their artifacts must certainly rate as great works of art of surpassing beauty.

133 The store huts of Nigeria are a study in themselves. The basic aim is of course simple: to keep the grain stored away from moisture and mice. The design and size varies from tribe to tribe. A store hut can be as reliable a guide as tribal marks or language. For details see René Gardi, *Indigenous African Architecture*.

135 There are several notable waterfalls that drop from the plateau. The easiest to view are the Assob Falls beside the road on the Jos–Wamba road, near the bottom of the drop-off of the plateau. Much grander, but more difficult of access, are the falls shown in this photograph. The Sha River meanders across the plateau through some lovely country to the south west of Daffo. It then begins a series of falls, the last and greatest of which is pictured here, and becomes the Farin Ruwa River. In the dry season excellent picnics and swims can be had in the upper reaches of the river.

To reach these falls, leave the Jos–Wamba road a few kilometres north of Wamba, drive along ever-narrowing tracks to the village of Mama and then to the site of the Marhai Rest House (9°07′N, 8°43′E; see sheet 44 of the 1:250,000 survey of Nigeria). Now with occasional glimpses of the waterfall walk for an hour across difficult terrain, which is virtually pathless, to reach the Farin Ruwa River. Following the river upstream needs care and some agility. For the very hardy, an additional four hours plus of climbing, scrambling and walking enables you to climb the whole falls complex (in the dry season) to the plateau and the track near Mistakuru. This last should only be attempted by the very fit. A car needs to be sent round, and the drive also takes four hours. A prior reconnaissance is recommended.

The Mama were one of Nigeria's fiercest hill tribes. In the mid-1920s it could still be written:

> No attention was paid by the war-like Mamas, secure in their hill-top fortresses, to official messages . . . it could be said that it had not yet been brought for practical purposes under any form of control. Government officials . . . (were) invariably accompanied by a police escort for their protection.

Today the Mama are less belligerent. But the walker becomes aware of their proud independence.

136–137 Hoss Peak (1534 m) and its surrounding valley are easily reached from Jos, 32 km away. It is a splendid place for picnics, hill walking and rock climbing and, during and just after the rainy season, for bird watching. With the air crisp and clear, there can be few better places to explore and enjoy in all Nigeria.

138–139 *Sukur, Kamale and the Mandara Mountains*
Sukur is a tiny, very remote mountain village which nevertheless has considerable history and a most beautiful setting. To get to Sukur turn south-eastwards off the main Bama–Mubi road at Chambula, some 12–13 km west-south-west of Madagali. Follow a goodish dirt track (not easily passable after rain, easy for all vehicles if moderately dry) for some 10 km to Mildo. Take the lesser right track in the middle of the village at the Y-junction (very faint) and continue for another 5 km along a rather poor rocky track (all sturdy cars can make it) until it ends at a schoolhouse. Leave the car here and, in Hausa, engage a guide. Walk for 1 km along the valley bottom and then start the climb on the easily graded stone causeway to Sukur, which makes the steep ascent much easier than expected. Allow 90 minutes from schoolhouse to Sukur. If the Llidi (or King), who is very hospitable, is to be interviewed, Hausa is essential. The stone causeway was built by slave labour in the days when Sukur was a power in the land. Cavalry would clatter down onto the plain from Sukur's mountain fastness to carry out a raid. (For full details of Sukur, see A. H. M. Kirk-Greene, 'The Kingdom of Sukur, a Northern Nigerian Ichabod', article in *Nigerian Field*, 1960.)

Kamale village is reached by taking a passable dirt road from Michika (on the main Bama–Mubi road). Only 1 km from the village is an astonishing vertical volcanic plug. The walk to near its base is uphill but not difficult, and the views are superlative. The plug is on the Cameroun frontier, but as the frontier is unmarked, villagers pass to and fro for market days.

The Mandara Mountains, which stretch from just south of the Bama–Mora road to well south of Mubi, provide some of the most spectacular scenery in all Africa. Enormous volcanic plugs rise vertically out of the plateau in the most astonishing manner.

A splendid week-long holiday can be had by making a circuit of the Mandara Mountains on both sides of the frontier (they run along

Nigeria's north-eastern frontier with Cameroun). The highlights of such a circuit, which would begin and end at Yola or Maiduguri, include the volcanic scenery around Kamale and Roumsiki, with a day at each place; a visit to Sukur; and the extraordinary descent to Mora (scene of Denham's disgrace, see Bibliography). The best time to undertake the journey is May.

140–141 The Mambilla Plateau, in south-eastern Gongola State, and lying along the Cameroun frontier, is arguably the most remote area in all Nigeria. The approach is either from Yola to the north or Takum to the west. The road winds into the valley around Serti before beginning the arduous climb up onto the plateau.

Once up you have entered a new world. The air is cool by day and cold by night. It is rich cattle country. The people are hardy and self-reliant. Gembu, in the heart of the plateau, provides an excellent base for walking in the hills to the south. And a walk along the northern edge of the scarp is a wonderful day's expedition. Altogether it is very well worth the effort of getting to Mambilla.

142–143 The man's horizontal narrow strip hand loom can be found over much of West Africa. Its size and mobility contrasts with the purely Nigerian woman's vertical loom, a much larger affair altogether (see 82 and 163). The narrow strips of cloth the men weave, and which can be many metres long, are cut up and sewn together.

The finest of all the work is done in Gongola, north of Yola, in Zummo and its surrounding villages. This gown is an example of this very fine Zummo work, which is highly prized throughout northern Nigeria. For further reading, see Lamb and Holmes, *Nigerian Weaving*.

144–149 No one is certain of the origin of the Fulani. One theory has it that in prehistoric times they migrated from Asia, across North Africa and down the western coast of Africa to the Senegal region; other theories, variants of the first, that they originated either in Upper Egypt or in the Berber areas of North Africa. What is generally accepted is that the forebears of the Fulani now living in northern Nigeria and bordering countries came from the Senegal basin to the west. Their arrival in Hausaland in the 13th century was gradual and peaceful.

Two distinct groups of Fulani emerged over time. Some abandoned the pastoral life and took to the towns, freely mingling with the Hausa inhabitants and adopting the Muslim religion; often they rose to high positions under the Hausa rulers. These were the Fulani Gidda ('Gidda' is a 'compound'). Others remained aloof, retaining their pastoral life and only marrying among themselves. These are the 'cow Fulani' or Borroro-je.

The Fulani were more or less a subject race in Hausaland for centuries. Then in 1804 Uthman dan Fodio, a Fulani scholar and holy man, raised the banner of revolt. Successful in battle against the pagan King of Gobir, a *jihad* or holy war was launched. Fulani clans flocked to his standard and named him Sarkin Musulmi, Commander of the Faithful. Uthman gave 'flags' to 14 chiefs, who were authorized to wage war in the name of Allah and His Prophet. For a time the Fulani seemed unbeatable, and the Emirates of Katsina, Kano, Zaria, Adamawa, Gombe, Daura, Nupe, Bauchi and Ilorin, among others, were soon established. Only Borno, under the inspired generalship of Al-Kanemi (see note 123 above), withstood the onslaught.

The *jihad* successful, dan Fodio divided his empire between his brother and his son Bello. He continued to study and preach in Sokoto, his son's capital, until his death in 1817. It was Bello, now Sarkin Musulmi, that Clapperton visited in 1824 and 1826.

Today's Emirs of the great northern cities of Nigeria are descendants of the original Fulani Emirs who overran the cities of northern Nigeria.

For the Borroro-je life remains largely unaltered. They speak their own language, they marry among themselves, they are proud and shy and self-sufficient, and their life centres on their herds of cattle. They are seen most commonly in the market places, for they love the whirl and gossip of market day. Their women sell the milk of their herds. Both sexes wear jewellery, often in profusion.

The Borroro-je place the highest priority on protecting their cattle; their second concern is to increase their numbers. They are outnumbered by the townspeople, and dread losing their own distinct culture. Alas, time and progress are not on their side. One day the great herds will no longer move across the north, protected by their unique owners.

150 Obudu Ranch (or Hotel) is a fine place to recuperate from the humidity of the lowlands. It lies in the very north of Cross River State, high on a plateau, a considerable distance from Obudu town. Routes to it start from Calabar in the south, Enugu in the west or Makurdi to the north, all easily driveable in a day. A newly built tarmac road leads up the mountain to the fine hotel. Splendid walking can be had along the ridges around Obudu. Evenings can be very cold.

152–155 Idah, with its strategic position high above the Niger River, is an ancient town whose beginning is shrouded in the mists of history. At some stage the Igale people formed a substantial state with its capital at Idah. The Atta (or King) of Idah controlled the left bank of the Niger for about 150 km below the confluence. In the 15th century it was on the fringes of the great empire of Benin. All the 19th-century travellers on the Niger remarked on Idah's beauty. Richard Lander was the first to see it, in 1830, and he commented:

> It is situated close to the water's edge . . . in an elevated situation, and on a fine greensward: its appearance was unspeakably beautiful. The town is clean, of prodigious extent, and ornamented with verdant shrubs and tall goodly trees. A few canoes were lying at the foot of the town.

The description fits just as well today. See the Bibliography for 19th-century Niger travellers.

156–157 The Tiv are a tough and sturdy race, industrious farmers, fishermen and hunters.

The harmattan season is the time of the north wind (November–April), which carries a haze of fine Saharan dust over all of Nigeria, and indeed West Africa.

158 above The University at Nsukka is one of the main Nigerian centres of learning. It was founded by Dr Nnamdi Azikiwe, the country's first President after Independence in 1960.

158 below The bridge at Onitsha is the main east–west artery across the lower Niger; the river provides the northwards passage. Inevitably Onitsha has become one of the largest of Nigerian markets.

159 In 1938 a man was digging a cistern in his new compound on the outskirts of Igbo-Ukwu, a town some 40 km south east of Onitsha. Less than a metre down he came across a highly decorated bronze bowl. The first proper excavation did not take place for another 20 years; the finds were rich, and included a royal burial chamber and a storehouse full of regalia. The site is provisionally dated to the 9th or 10th century AD. For further details see Thurstan Shaw, *Igbo-Ukwu* (2 vols) or his much shorter *Unearthing Igbo-Ukwu*; and Ekpo Eyo, *Two Thousand Years Nigerian Art*.

161 The Aro tribe dominated trade in its area for several centuries by virtue of the awe in which an important oracle was held. This oracle, which was controlled by the Aros, was the Long Juju of Aro Chuku. The Aros were not a warlike people, but with the Long Juju as a severe and final sanction they cleverly played one tribe off against another. All disputes were settled by reference to the oracle, which was housed in a cave. The loser disappeared in the cave and was believed by his tribe to have been destroyed by the hidden power. In reality, unconscious and bound, he was smuggled out of a back entrance and sold into slavery. The Aros give fresh evidence of their intelligence when the Long Juju was subdued by the British; they immediately accepted the imposed conditions and took advantage of the increased trade caused by the opening up of their country. For further details see P. A. Talbot, *The Peoples of Southern Nigeria* and E. Isichei, *A History of the Igbo People*.

163 'Akwete is probably the most famous of all places associated with the use of the woman's vertical loom in Nigeria.'

The craft of weaving continues to thrive in Akwete, and its cloths are highly prized by women throughout southern Nigeria. See also 82 and 142–143. For further details see Lamb and Holmes, *Nigerian Weaving*, chapter 10.

164–165 Stone sculptures representing the human figure are surprisingly rare in West Africa. Those of Sierra Leone, the Bakongo and of Esie in northern Yorubaland are mainly in steatite, which can be worked almost as easily as wood. The two remaining groups are the carvings at Ife and its surrounds, which are in a hard crystalline rock but total fewer than a dozen; and the extraordinary group of nearly 300 granite sculptures in a relatively remote area in eastern Nigeria.

These are the Akwanshi of the Ekoi people. The pre-Cambrian granite, which lies exposed in stream beds, and from which the Akwanshi are carved, is very hard and must have required much labour. Not a great deal is known about them, but the earliest may date from the 16th century. Several good examples are now in the grounds of Lagos Museum, while many others remain *in situ*. For further details, see P. Allison, *Cross River Monoliths*.

168–171 Nembe dates from about the 13th century, when a wave of emigration from Benin led to isolated settlements in various parts of the Delta. The fortunes of Nembe flowed and ebbed over the centuries, leading to a spreading of its people; this was in particular so after a disastrous civil war in the 15th century. The drum title of Nembe is 'Ama doko doko biokpo', which means 'the small but very brave city-state'.

The coronation of its Mingi or King is a grand affair and was celebrated in 1980 with the accession of Mingi XI. A major part of the celebrations on the second day are the visits by war canoes of the new king to each compound in the town, to secure the acknowledgement of that compound to the new ruler.

172 Port Harcourt did not exist until 1913, when work began building a harbour and railway from Port Harcourt to northern Nigeria. Because of World War I and operations by the British against the Germans in Cameroun, it quickly became a major town. It acquired renewed importance as the centre of the oil industry operations from 1960 onwards.

173 The straight seismic lines cut through the mangrove swamp. This is oil country *par excellence*, and a flare burning off unwanted associated gas testifies to oil production in the area.

174 above The bitter gourd (*Momordica charantia*), up-country western Oyo in light secondary forest.

174 below The flower of a 20 m African tulip tree (*Spathodea campanulata*), on a hill behind Lokoja. The 10 cm flowers can be seen in September and October.

175 Dardanus swallowtail (*Papilio dardanus*) fluttering over the flowers of a clerodendron bush (*Clerodendrum speciosissimum*).

176 above left Fire-crowned bishop (*Euplectes hordeaceus*) in Hoss Valley, Plateau State.

176 above right Carmine bee-eater (*Merops nubicus*) near Bama, Borno State.

176 below Pin-tailed whydah (*Vidua macroura*) near Yola, Gongola State.

177 Bateleur (*Terathopius ecaudatus*) near Biu, Borno State.

178 above Female golden orb weaver spider (*Nephila constricta*, genus Argiopidae), Anambra State.

178 below Variegated grasshopper (*Zonocerus variegatus*) at Zaria.

179 Mating Angola white lady swallowtails (*Graphium pylades*), Benue State.

180 left The large red laterite mounds seen in the bush are formed by termite colonies which consist of millions of individuals in an 'organized' community. There are specialized groups that act as soldiers or workers and a single queen is responsible for the reproduction of the colony. The nest is below ground; the visible tower or mound is probably for ventilation purposes.

181 above An African beauty snake (*Psammophis sibilams*) sunning itself in a bush.

181 below A Forest cobra (*Naja melanoleuca*) in its banded phase, more than 2 m long.

186–187 The search for oil began in 1937, but the pioneers (the predecessors of what is today the Shell Petroleum Development Company of Nigeria) had many disappointments before the first commercial discovery was made in 1956. The first cargo of crude oil was exported two years later. Intensification of the search for oil led to many further discoveries, for Nigerian oil accumulations are typically in a large number of small to medium fields rather than in a few large ones as in the Middle East. To date, the fields have all been in or around the Niger Delta area, on land, in the swamps and offshore.

Today the Nigerian National Petroleum Corporation owns a majority shareholding in the production acreage, with foreign oil companies owning the minority share of these joint ventures. Production capacity is some two million barrels of crude per day, which makes Nigeria both one of the world's leading producing countries and also a major member of OPEC. Nigeria has even more gas than oil, and no doubt this will become a significant foreign currency earner in the not too distant future. Crude oil income represents over 90% of Nigerian foreign earnings today. There are sufficient reserves of oil and gas to ensure that Nigeria will remain a significant exporter of hydrocarbons well into the next century.

BIBLIOGRAPHY

Ajayi, J.F.A., and Crowder, M. (eds)
History of West Africa, *London 1974 (2 vols)*

Ajayi, J.F.A., and Smith, R.
Yoruba Warfare in the Nineteenth Century, *Cambridge 1964*

Allen, W.
Picturesque Views of the River Niger, *London 1840*

Allen, W., and Thomson, T.R.H.
A Narrative of the Expedition to the Niger River in 1841, *London 1848 (2 vols)*

Allison, P.
Cross River Monoliths, *Lagos 1968*

Anene, J.C.
The International Boundaries of Nigeria, *London 1970*

Baikie, W.B.
Narrative of an Exploring Voyage up the Rivers Kwora and Binue in 1854, *London 1856*

Barth, H.
Travels and Discoveries in North and Central Africa, *London 1858 (5 vols)*

Bascom, W.
The Yoruba of Southeastern Nigeria, *New York 1969*

Basden, G.T.
Niger Ibos, *London 1938*

Beier, U.
The Return of the Gods, *Cambridge 1975*

Biobaku, S.O.
The Egba and their Neighbours 1832–1872, *London 1957*

Biobaku, S.O.
Sources of Yoruba History, *Oxford 1973*

Birks, J.S.
Across the Savannas to Mecca, *London 1978*

Boahen, A.A.
Britain, the Sahara and the Western Sudan, 1788–1861, *Oxford 1964*

Bovill, E.W. (ed)
Missions to the Niger, *Cambridge 1964–6 (4 vols)*

Bovill, E.W.
The Golden Trade of the Moors, *Oxford 1968*

Bovill, E.W.
The Niger Explored, *London 1968*

Bowen, T.J.
Adventures and Missionary Labours in the Interior of Africa, *Charleston 1857*

Bradbury, R.E.
The Benin Kingdom and the Edo-speaking Peoples of South-Western Nigeria, *London 1970*

Brenner, L.
The Shehus of Kukawa. A History of the Al-Kanem Dynasty of Bornu, *Oxford 1973*

Brent, P.
Black Nile, *London 1977*

Burns, A.C.
History of Nigeria, *London 1929*

Chappel, T.J.H.
Decorated Gourds in North-Eastern Nigeria, *Lagos 1977*

Clapperton, H.
Journal of a Second Expedition into the Interior of Africa, *London 1829 (2 vols)*

Clarke, W.H.
Travels and Explorations in Yorubaland (1854–58), *Ibadan 1972*

Crowder, M.
The Story of Nigeria, *London 1962*

Crowther, S.A.
Journal of an Expedition up the Niger and Tshadda Rivers . . . in 1854, *London 1855*

Denham, D., Clapperton, H., and Oudney, W.
Narrative of Travels and Discoveries in Northern and Central Africa, *London 1826*

Egharevba, J.
A Short History of Benin, *Ibadan 1960*

Enahoro, P.
How to be a Nigerian, *Ibadan 1966*

Eyo, Ekpo
Two Thousand Years Nigerian Art, *Lagos 1977*

Fagg, B.
Nok Terracottas, *Lagos 1977*

Forde, D. (ed)
Ethnographic Survey of Africa: Western Africa, *London 1950–69*

Frobenius, L.
The Voice of Africa, *London 1913 (2 vols)*

Gardi, R.
Indigenous African Architecture, *London 1973*

Gramont, S. de
The Strong Brown God – The Story of the Niger River, *London 1975*

Hallet, R. (ed)
The Niger Journal of Richard and John Lander, *London 1965*

Hallet, R.
The Penetration of Africa to 1815, *London 1965*

Hill, P.
Rural Hausa, *Cambridge 1972*

Hodder, B.W., and Ukwu, U.I.
Markets in West Africa, *Ibadan 1969*

Hodgkin, T. (ed)
Nigerian Perspectives, *London 1960*

Hopen, C.E.
The Pastoral Fulbe Family in Gwandu, *Oxford 1959*

Isichei, E.
A History of the Igbo People, *London 1976*

Johnson, S.
The History of the Yorubas, *Lagos 1921*

Kingsley, M.
West African Studies, *London 1899*

Kirk-Greene, A.H.M.
Barth's Travels in Nigeria, *London 1962*

Laird, Macgregor, and Oldfield, R.A.K.
Narrative of an Expedition into the Interior of Africa, *London 1837 (2 vols)*

Lamb, V., and Holmes, J.
Nigerian Weaving, *Lagos 1980*

Lander, R.
Records of Captain Clapperton's Last Expedition to Africa, *London 1830 (2 vols)*

Last, M.
The Sokoto Caliphate, *Ibadan 1967*

Law, R.
The Oyo Empire, 1600–1836, *Oxford 1977*

Meek, C.K.
The Northern Tribes of Nigeria, *London 1925 (2 vols)*

Nadel, S.F.
A Black Byzantium, *Oxford 1942*

Palmer, H.R. (ed)
Sudanese Memoirs, *Lagos 1928 (3 vols)*

Perham, M.
Lugard, *London 1956 (2 vols)*

Ryder, A.
Benin and the Europeans 1485–1897, *Ibadan 1967*

St Croix, F.W. de
The Fulani of Northern Nigeria, *Lagos 1944*

St Jorre, J. de
The Nigerian Civil War, *London 1972*

Schultze, A.
The Sultanate of Bornu, *London 1913*

Shaw, T.C.
Igbo-Ukwu, *London 1970 (2 vols)*

Shaw, T.C.
Unearthing Igbo-Ukwu, *Ibadan 1977*

Stremlau, J.J.
The International Politics of the Nigerian Civil War, *Princeton 1977*

Talbot, P.A.
The Peoples of Southern Nigeria, *Oxford 1926 (4 vols)*

Temple, O.
Notes on the Tribes, Provinces, Emirates and States of the Northern Provinces of Nigeria, *London 1919*

Trimingham, J.S.
Islam in West Africa, *Oxford 1959*

Zaria Field Society
Guide to the Zaria Area, *Zaria 1978 (3rd ed)*

Natural History

Bannerman, D.A.
The Birds of West and Equatorial Africa, *London 1953 (2 vols)*

Gledhill, D.
West African Trees, *London 1972*

Serle, W., and Morel, G.J.
A Field Guide to the Birds of West Africa, *London 1977*

Williams, J.G.
A Field Guide to the Butterflies of Africa, *London 1973*

INDEX